Tamm's Textbook

AP* U.S. History student workbook containing vocabulary and chapter assignments to use with:

Kennedy, Cohen, and Bailey's

The American Pageant⁺

16th edition (red, white & blue cover)

Coursepak Series A   **Independently Made**

David Tamm

For the 3%

Copyright © 2016

CONTENTS

This resource book is organized in the following way to integrate with *The American Pageant:*

Suggested Year and Weekly Plan

Vocab and Chapter Assignments

Addenda: Crash Course, Test Correction Forms, Movie Review Forms & More

LICENSING

When given as a full workbook, this material improves content coherency, student enjoyment, parent appreciation, and teacher satisfaction. "

-State of Florida Certified Teacher

"Sublimely usable."

"Great as weekly assignments"

"Spend one hour's pay, save 300 hours' planning time!"

"Rocket into the

"Textbooks are expensive. With this workbook, you get your money's worth!"

frontier of utility!"

"They read the book, which is the main issue many have."

"Perfect if there's a substitute"

"Very progressive."

Suggested Year Plan

The ongoing issue with *The American Pageant* is its number of chapters. Most schools begin in late August or early September, leaving ~30 weeks to get through the book if you want any time for review before the exam. Yet there are 41 chapters in the 16th edition of the *Pageant* book, down from 47 in the original 1956 edition, but still not whittled down enough to fit a standard-length course, especially if you want to enjoy the semblance of military-style structure. This means it is up to the individual teacher to combine 10 or so chapters. Some give out that amount as a summer assignment. But if you can't or don't do that, know that the period before Jamestown and the period after 1980 only constitute 5% of the test each. What follows is the book contents, and a blast from the past of how this course was ordered when it was young.

<table>
<tr><td colspan="3">The American Pageant 16th edition
Bailey/Kennedy/Cohen, 2016
Weekly Breakdown</td><td>A History of Our Country
David S. Muzzey, 1942
Flashback</td></tr>
<tr><td>Week 1: Ch. 1</td><td>New World Beginnings</td><td></td><td>Europe Wakes and Stretches</td></tr>
<tr><td>Week 2: Ch. 2</td><td>The Planting of English America</td><td></td><td>A Century of Exploration</td></tr>
<tr><td>Week 3: Ch. 3</td><td>Settling the Northern Colonies</td><td></td><td>The English Settlements</td></tr>
<tr><td>Week 4: Ch. 4</td><td>American Life in the 17th Century</td><td></td><td>Colonial America</td></tr>
<tr><td>Week 5: Ch. 5</td><td>Colonial Society on the Eve</td><td></td><td>Liberty or Loyalty?</td></tr>
<tr><td>Week 6: Ch. 6</td><td>The Duel for North America</td><td></td><td>Washington Sees it Through</td></tr>
<tr><td>Week 7: Ch. 7</td><td>The Road to Revolution</td><td></td><td>Confederation and Constitution</td></tr>
<tr><td>Week 8: Ch. 8</td><td>America Secedes from the Empire</td><td></td><td>Launching the Government</td></tr>
<tr><td>Week 9: Ch. 9</td><td>Confederation and Constitution</td><td></td><td>Jefferson makes a Great Bargain</td></tr>
<tr><td>Week 10: Ch. 10</td><td>Launching the New Ship of State</td><td></td><td>Our Second War for Independence</td></tr>
<tr><td>Week 11: Ch. 11</td><td>The Jeffersonian Republic</td><td></td><td>Sectional Rivalry</td></tr>
<tr><td>Week 12: Ch. 12</td><td>Second War for Independence</td><td></td><td>The Jacksonian Era</td></tr>
<tr><td>Week 13: Ch. 13</td><td>The Rise of Mass Democracy</td><td></td><td>Advance to the Pacific</td></tr>
<tr><td>Week 14: Ch. 14</td><td>Forging the National Economy</td><td></td><td>The Businessman's Peace</td></tr>
<tr><td>Week 15: Ch. 15</td><td>Ferment of Reform and Culture</td><td></td><td>The House Divided</td></tr>
<tr><td>Week 16: Ch. 16</td><td>The South and Slavery</td><td></td><td>The Civil War</td></tr>
<tr><td>Week 17: Ch. 17</td><td>Manifest Destiny and Its Legacy</td><td></td><td>Reconstruction</td></tr>
<tr><td>Week 18: Ch. 18</td><td>Renewing the Sectional Struggle</td><td></td><td>The New Industrial Age</td></tr>
<tr><td>Week 19: Ch. 19</td><td>Drifting Towards Disunion</td><td></td><td>Futile Party Battles</td></tr>
<tr><td>Week 20: Ch. 20</td><td>Girding for War: North and South</td><td></td><td>The Rising of the West</td></tr>
<tr><td>Week 21: Ch. 21</td><td>The Furnace of Civil War</td><td></td><td>Dominion Over Palm and Pine</td></tr>
<tr><td>Week 22: Ch. 22</td><td>The Ordeal of Reconstruction</td><td></td><td>The Roosevelt Era</td></tr>
<tr><td>Week 23: Ch. 23</td><td>Political Paralysis in the Gilded Age</td><td></td><td>The Progressive Movement</td></tr>
<tr><td>Week 24: Ch. 24</td><td>Industry Comes of Age</td><td></td><td>Wilson and the 'New Freedom'</td></tr>
<tr><td>Week 25: Ch. 25</td><td>America Moves to the City</td><td></td><td>The Struggle for Neutrality</td></tr>
<tr><td>Week 26: Ch. 26</td><td>The Great West and Agriculture</td><td></td><td>Our Part in the Fighting</td></tr>
<tr><td>Week 27: Ch. 27</td><td>Empire and Expansion</td><td></td><td>Influence of the War on Life</td></tr>
<tr><td>Week 28: Ch. 28</td><td>Progressivism and Roosevelt</td><td></td><td>Our Part in the Peace</td></tr>
<tr><td>Week 29: Ch. 29</td><td>Wilsonian Progressivism and War</td><td></td><td>The Aftermath of the War</td></tr>
<tr><td>Week 30: Ch. 30</td><td>American Life in the Roaring '20s</td><td></td><td>The Program of 'Normalcy'</td></tr>
<tr><td>Week 31: Ch. 31</td><td>The Politics of Boom and Bust</td><td></td><td>Worshipping the Golden Calf</td></tr>
<tr><td>Week 32: Ch. 32</td><td>Great Depression and New Deal</td><td></td><td>The Eclipse of Prosperity</td></tr>
<tr><td>Week 33: Ch. 33</td><td>FDR and the Shadow of War</td><td></td><td>The 'Hundred Days'</td></tr>
<tr><td>Week 34: Ch. 34</td><td>American in WWII</td><td></td><td>The New Deal on Trial</td></tr>
<tr><td>Week 35: Ch. 35</td><td>The Cold War Begins</td><td></td><td>Entering a New Decade</td></tr>
<tr><td>Week 36: Ch. 36</td><td>American Zenith</td><td></td><td></td></tr>
<tr><td>Week 37: Ch. 37</td><td>The Stormy Sixties</td><td></td><td></td></tr>
<tr><td>Week 38: Ch. 38</td><td>Challenges to the Postwar Order</td><td></td><td></td></tr>
<tr><td>Week 39: Ch. 39</td><td>The Resurgence of Conservatism</td><td></td><td></td></tr>
<tr><td>Week 40: Ch. 40</td><td>Confronting the Post-Cold War Era</td><td></td><td></td></tr>
<tr><td>Week 41: Ch. 41</td><td>Facing a New Century</td><td></td><td></td></tr>
</table>

Suggested Weekly Plan

Manic Moon Day

It is recommended that students have a lecture overview of the key points in each chapter, take notes, and discuss the concepts involved. Even though teachers are discouraged in parts of the country from lecturing, the speed of the AP* U.S. History course necessitates some direct teacher-student transmission of content. The chapter assignment forms presented herein could be used as a guide during the discussion.

Textbook Tiw's Day

Most school districts encourage pair or group work. This can be used to positive effect if students mine the textbook (or a review book) in class and either jigsaw the chapter, presenting their take on part of the whole, or jointly venture to find the answers to the specific problems in history. The activities herein lend themselves to this kind of classroom setting too. Groups can, for example, take part of each chapter assignment and focus on that, and then discuss their part whole group.

Writing Woden's Day

The AP* U.S. History curriculum is reading and writing intensive, and brainstorming (diagramming) solutions to mini-FRQs is a good way to build up key thinking processes helpful in expressing oneself in writing. Another helpful way is practicing good old-fashioned reading comprehension, but as many teachers know, the content of the passages is key to student growth and success. The material has to be interesting, and luckily, U.S. History has a great potential interest value. If you find the current materials helpful and of high enough quality, you may want to obtain the companion volume to this book, *Tamm's Textbook Tools Coursepak Series B: Reading Shorts, Writings and Online Activities*, on *Amazon.com* or another platform.

Technetronic Thor's Day

Many AP* teachers try to bring in technology to the classroom, whether in the form of a laptop cart, or by taking students to a media lab. Increasingly, students are using their own mobile devices. *Kahoot.it* is now popular as a Jeopardy-style review game, joining *Quizlet* and a vast number of other review materials available online. A good directory to websites usable with AP U.S. History classes, including the Bailey textbook site with history activities, is located at Antarcticaedu.com/US.htm. Included in the addendum to this volume is a Crash Course viewer response sheet that can be given as homework on Thursday nights, or completed as an in-class review assignment.

Fantastic Frija's Day

It is suggested that students take a 25-50-question test once a week. That means a couple chapters might have to be doubled up. A timed, 35 min. period should be reserved in class- or in some cases out depending on how nice you are- to do a weekly 50 question test. If this happens on Friday, it is recommended students take home the chapter assignments for the next week's chapter, or at least part of it, for homework. Doing just the vocab, for example, is itself is a good way to introduce a new chapter.

Now let's get down to business!

Manic Monday

and

Textbook Tuesday

Chapter Activities

Quote 4: To the king and queen of which country is Columbus speaking? _____(pg. 14)

Graph 5: Choose the longer period in time:

   a. From Columbus to the founding of Virginia   *b. From Virginia to Independence*

If the Colonial era was 169 years long, how long has it been *since* independence? _____

The oldest mountains in the Americas are: _____

Canadian Shield _____

'Tidewater' _____

'Roof of America' _____

Did glaciers cover *your* state during the Ice Age? _____

Describe the process by which the Great Lakes formed: The Great Lakes are easily recalled by the mnemonic device HOMES:

_____

_____ H   M

_____ O   E

                        S

_____ is the 'leftover' lake that is the remnant of Lake Bonneville.

Bering Strait _____

The migrant ancestors of the Indians: *a. arrived all at one time* *b. arrived over centuries*

_____

Map 6: During the Ice Age there was *a. more* *b. less* land than there is today.

Recalling the water cycle from science class, why do you think this is so? Where *was* the water?

_____

Incas _____

Mayans _____

Aztecs (Mexica) _____

Maize _____

Map 7: Munster's map dates from the year _____.

Name three islands marked in the Caribbean Sea:	North America is distorted and its size is
	a. too small b. too large

| Pic 8: This 'corn god' is from the Moche culture of Peru. Which major culture lived in Peru after the Moche? | Describe how the Aztecs honored their gods: |
| | _____ |

Pueblo _____

Nation-State _____

Mound-Builders _____

Cahokia _____

Anasazi _____

Three-sister farming _____

Hiawatha _____

Describe the basic lifestyle of the native peoples of North America:

Map 9: Relate the names of the tribes in each region:

Arctic & Subarctic	Northwest Coast	California	Plateau

Great Plains	Great Basin	Northeast	Southwest

Which tribes are nearest to the part of the country you live?	The overall population in 1492 is estimated to have been:
	_____
	Is that more or less than in your *state*?

Pic 10: Sketch out the broad outlines of Cahokia at right, and Be sure to include the central building, lakes, etc.:

The large U.S. city closest to Cahokia's earthen mound, is: _____

Why do historians believe Leif Eriksson and the Scandinavian Vikings arrived on the shores of 'Vinland' 500 years before Columbus? Why didn't they stay?

Map 11: What does the orange area on the map signify?	Which European explorer made it to India to establish a trade route for spices?
_____	_____

List the major spices Europeans were looking for: _____

Middlemen

Caravel

Pic 12: Marco Polo is shown in a caravel, what animals did he bring with him?	Pic 13: Why did they call this the 'Door of No Return?'
_____	_____
Why did the Arab slave traders sell captives caught far away for higher prices?	Why did slave brokers mix people from different regions?

Plantation

'Dark Continent'

Ferdinand of Aragon

Isabella of Castile

Islamic forces from North Africa conquered much of Spain in 711. Christians called the eventual driving out of the Muslims the *'Reconquista,'* accomplished by Ferdinand and Isabella in 1492. Why did they 'buy in' to Columbus outlandish idea of sailing directly out into the ocean sea?

Christopher Columbus

Columbus was from this place: *He thought he was going to:*   *He arrived in the Americas on:*

The diffusion of crops and animals from one side of the world to the other is called the **Columbian Exchange**. List some of the things brought from each side of the world to the other:

From Old World to New   *From New World to Old*

'Sugar revolution'

Pic 15: The disease that killed many more Aztecs than guns and swords was _____

Contending Voices 16 - Summarize the views of the following:

Juan Gines de Sepulveda   *Bartolome de Las Casas*

With whom do you agree more?

Treaty of Tordesillas

Encomienda _____

Hernan Cortes _____

Malinche (Dona Marina) _____

Tenochtitlan _____

Conquistador _____

Moctezuma _____

Quetzalcoatl _____

Noche triste _____

Mexico City _____

Map 17: Note the major geographical places reached by the following explorers/conquistadors:

Columbus: *Cabot:*   *Balboa:*

Vespucci: *De Leon:*   *Cabeza de Vaca:*

Pizzaro: *Coronado:*   *De Soto:*

Pg. 19: What are some of the things the Spanish Conquistadors did to become 'Makers of America?'

_____

_____

_____

Capitalism _____

Mestizos _____

Dia de la Raza _____

Pic 20: This large city called _____, was built by the _____.

(This space intentionally left empty. Feel free to doodle →)

Polytheism is the belief in many gods, monotheism is the belief in one God, and atheism is the belief in none. Which of these three best characterizes the Mesoamericans?

Summarize the *tools* used by the Spaniards to defeat the Aztecs:

_____

Map 21: While Ponce de Leon searched for the Fountain of Youth and found Florida (to which many elderly people go today to seek a healthy and youth-inspiring climate), what was Coronado searching for and what did he find instead?

_____

Battle of Ancona _____

Pope's Rebellion _____

Kiva _____

Robert de la Salle _____

Black Legend _____

Map 22: The Battle of Ancona took place the modern state of _____

Mission San Antonio is on the _____ side of the   What year was El Paso founded?
Rio Grande River, meaning it is in modern day Texas.

                                                              _____

Mission _____

Junipero Serra _____

Pic 22: What was the fate of Dona Marina- what did she do after her famous translations?

_____

What does the term 'collision of cultures' mean to you after having read all this?

_____

If we name our first colony on Mars after Captain Kirk, will it be called Jamestown too?

Quote 25: What was Walter Raleigh determined to do?

_____

Protestant Reformation _____

Henry VIII _____

Elizabeth I _____

Buccaneers _____

Table 26: The Tudor monarchs were, in order:

Sir Francis Drake _____

Sir Walter Raleigh _____

Pic 26: One reason this is called the "Armada Portrait" is because of its effective use of propaganda portraying the queen as a serene, sovereign power in her own right. Speaking of right, what does she have underneath her right hand? What do you think this means?

_____

_____

Roanoke Island _____

The Spanish Armada _____

Pg. 27 Contending Voices:

Hakluyt's View: **Percy's View:**

_____

What do you think accounts for the difference in the views of Hakluyt and Percy?

_____

William Shakespeare called England the _____. How did *enclosure* affect the country socially?

Primogeniture _____

Joint-Stock Company _____

Pic 28: Sir Walter Raleigh wrote one of the first world history books of modern times while he was in prison in the Tower of London. Why was the queen so mad at him?

_____

Virginia Company _____

Charter _____

Jamestown _____

Describe some of the challenges the Jamestown colonists faced when they arrived in 1607:	Why does the book say the buzzards made out well?

Captain John Smith _____

The first 'law' made by the English in North America was:

"He who shall not _____, shall not _____." What is your opinion on this law?

_____

Map 29: At right, sketch the craggy coast of Chesapeake Bay and place the English settlements of the 17th century:

Pic 29: Relate the story of Pocahontas, her background, significance in history, and what became of her:

_____

_____

_____

_____

Powhatan

Lord De La Warr

1st Anglo-Powhatan War

2nd Anglo-Powhatan War

Pic 30: The gift this Indian girl got from the Europeans was:	The Powhatan's lost out because they fell to the "Three D's." These were:
_____	1)
Pic 31: Describe the *function* of the trade goods obtained in this picture by the Yuchi:	2)
	3)

Describe the effect on Indian life of the following:

Horses: *Disease:*   *Firearms:*

Pic 32: If you were down and out looking for a job in the nearest big city to you, and saw this ad in a window today, offering voyages and jobs in the following faraway lands, would you consider going?			
Western Australia:	*Definitely*	*Maybe*	*No*
Antarctica:	*Definitely*	*Maybe*	*No*
Colony on the Moon:	*Definitely*	*Maybe*	*No*

John Rolfe

Tobacco

Some nicknames for tobacco were:	The first transport of Africans to Virginia was in the year:

House of Burgesses

What was King James' opinion of the House of Burgesses?   How did he act on this opinion?

Lord Baltimore

Maryland was established as a safe place for: *Puritans*   *Anglicans*   *Catholics*

The workers brought over to work on Maryland's tobacco farms were primarily:	What did it mean to be 'indentured?'

Act of Toleration

Some Americans still today argue that America 'is a Christian country.' If you were a lawyer, how might you use the circumstances surrounding the Act of Toleration as evidence of the following:

America is (or was) a Christian country	*America is not (or was not) a Christian country*

Pic 34: Why was sugarcane considered a 'rich man's crop' as opposed to tobacco, the 'poor man's crop?	How does this picture support that idea?

Quote 34: Describe the punishment schedule for African slaves on Barbados in the 17th century:

Barbados Slave Code

The Stuart king _____ was (rather shockingly) executed by _____.

After a decade or so, the Stuart dynasty was restored when _____ was made king. How did the restoration of the Stuarts influence the colonizing of the Carolinas?

Charles Town (Charleston)

Squatters

Map 36: This river formed the border between the Carolina and Georgia colonies _____

Tuscarora War

What does it mean to say that Georgia was a 'buffer colony?'

James Oglethorpe

Savannah

Pg. 38: What are some of the things the Iroquois did to become 'Makers of America?'

Go back to pg. 35 and copy the essentials on the chart (what you thought you wouldn't have to?) ☺

	Colony Name	Founded by	Year	Status in 1775
1				
2				
3				
4				
5				
6				
7				
8				
9				
10				
11				
12				
13				

Better grab your Penn and get started Pilgrim, or you'll be Quakin', 'cause the Acts of Toleration don't cover sloth! Seriously. They don't.

Calvinism _____

Institutes of the Christian Religion _____

Predestination _____

Conversion _____

'Visible saints' _____

Puritans _____

Separatists _____

Pilgrims _____

Mayflower _____

Pic 43: Restored to its original, stark look, describe how you would feel living at the Plymouth Plantation, the first colony in New England:	Sketch it out in mini-rough draft form:

Myles Standish _____

Plymouth Rock _____

Mayflower Compact _____

Quote 44: What is the meaning of William Bradford's words in plain English?

_____

Thanksgiving Day _____

The Plymouth Colony can best be described as   *a. a Christian colony*   *b. economically attractive*

In America today in your opinion, if a group of people get together and want to start a colony like Plymouth, and have their own specific ethnic, religious or political composition, should they be allowed to? Why or why not?

_____

Massachusetts Bay Company

Great English Migration

John Winthrop

What do you think Winthrop meant by the statement that America "shall be as a city upon a hill?"

What did male property holders able to do that the rest of the Bay Colony was not?

Map 45 (left): List the names of the shires of England from which most of the Puritans set out:

Chances are if you look at a map of Massachusetts, you will find all these names there too:

a. true   b. false   c. never saw an atlas

Map 45 (right): The destinations in the Americas of the most British migrants in order of volume are:

Protestant Ethic

'Blue Law'

How did the poem *Day of Doom* describe the fate of the damned?

| How might the rules at your school change if it came under Puritan administration?

Quakers

Antinomianism

Pic 46: List some ways in which Anne Hutchinson was a tough and defiant lady:

| What terrible fate awaited her in the end?

Roger Williams

Rhode Island's capital is called 'Providence.'
What was the meaning of this to the settlers?

| Note reasons other settles found the
| Connecticut River valley attractive:
|
|
|

Fundamental Orders

Map 48: Sketch out and label the colored blobs representing the New England colonies, note the years of establishment, include the rivers that run through them, and dot the towns:

Wampanoag

Massasoit

Pequot War

Pic 49: Why did the Puritan militia and their Narragansett allies attack the Pequot Fort as shown?

Metacom (King Philip)

King Philip's War

How many English settlements were
burned down during King Philip's War?

| What fate awaited Metacom?
|
|
|

New England Confederation

English Civil War

Why were Bay Colony authorities upset with
King Charles II in the 1680s?

| Why was the Dominion of New England concept
| also disliked by the Bay Colony's leaders?
|
|
|
|

Table 50: Note the sovereigns of the Stuart dynasty in England and their relation to America:

1

2

I

3

4

5

Navigation Laws

Sir Edmund Andros

Glorious Revolution

Document 51: Find in the document five words that if you wrote them the way they are there in your English class, your teacher would mark wrong and how you would correct it:

	Old fashioned spelling/grammar	*How you would correct it*
1		
2		
3		
4		
5		

Map 51: The most significant thing to come out of the Dominion of New England concept was:

a. Andros foreshadowed the despotic rule of later kings   *b. It was the first time colonies were unified*

'Salutary neglect'

Summarize some reasons the Dutch Republic of the Netherlands experienced a little golden age in the 17th century:

Henry Hudson

Dutch West India Company

Map 52: At right, make a rough sketch of the various Colonies, label the rivers and geographical features, Note the names of the Indian tribes in the area, and

dot the towns:

Most modern observers would call the deal whereby the Dutch bought Manhattan Island from the local Indians:

    a. fair and square   *b. a total rip-off*

Before it was called New York City, it was called:

Patroonships

Peter Stuyvesant

Pic 53: The woman pictured probably obtained her dress, jewelry, fan and rug from

a. trade with the Bay Colony   *b. trade with local Indians*   *c. Dutch East Indian Company merchants*

Why was the original wall that gave its name to modern Wall Street built?

Describe why the Swedish colony in Delaware ended:	Instant karma: describe why the Dutch colony ended:

Pic 54: The departing Dutch ships are flying the flag of the Netherlands. Match the pattern:

Top stripe	Blue
Middle stripe	Red
Bottom stripe	White

Note the Anglicized place names around NYC:

    Haarlem _____

    Breuckelen _____

    Hellegat _____

Why'd Quakers 'quake'? (You always wanted to know; you just didn't know you wanted to know):

Society of Friends

Pic 55: Adjectives that describe the Quaker lifestyle. Ready go:

_____

William Penn

_____

Pic 56: Did 'Penn's Woodland' with its City of Brotherly Love (also known as _____)
live up to its promise of openness to differences in settlers and good relations with the Indians? If
you were a lawyer arguing yes and then no, what would be your 'exhibits' and evidence?

Yes it did   *No it didn't*

_____

Daily Double! What state was named after Lord De La Warr? _____
(Your prize? You're only a few questions away from being done with this chapter assignment)

You may remember from World History class (ah... the memories... loved that class!) that the
ancient river valleys attracted the first settled civilizations, such as the Sumerians, Egyptians,
Harappan Indians and Ancient Chinese. How did rivers play a similar role in America?

_____

What do you think the textbook authors mean when they say the Middle Colonies represent'd a
'Middle Way?'

_____

Pg. 58: Examining the Evidence. What about American history does this item illuminate?

_____

_____

Pg. 59: Varying Viewpoints. If you were a lawyer convincing a jury of the following, what evidence would you bring up to support your argument?

America is a branch of European culture   **America is its own unique culture**

_____

"If you don't get your head-right and brush those teeth, you're going to get the kind of indenture that doesn't go away!" –Colonial Mom

Quote 62: Bradford does not expressly list this as something afflicting the Pilgrims:

   a. lack of friends   *b. lack of shelter*   *c. tiredness*   *d. lack of clothing*

Life in the early Chesapeake was: *a. really, really tough*   *b. relaxing*

Indentured servants _____

Head-right system _____

Pic 63: Just about the first product that were specifically advertised to target markets was:

Quote 63: The companyman compares Virginia to the: *a. best   b. worst*   parts of England.

William Berkeley _____

Nathanial Bacon _____

Bacon's Rebellion _____

Contending Voices 64 – How did each think about the relationship between rulers and ruled:

    Nathanial Bacon   *William Berkeley*

Who do you agree with more?

_____

Examining the Evidence 65 - What did this deal entail?

_____

_____

Thinking Globally 66 – How many Africans died aboard ship or at sea on the way to the Americas? What were the primary cash crops those who lived worked on upon arriving?

_____

Africa has suffered with slavery as perhaps no other continent. To the vast unknown number of people throughout the centuries who have lived as slaves in Africa, add the total number of Africans kidnapped and taken between 700 and 1600 from the East Coast to the Middle East, primarily by Arab slave traders (~12,000,000), to the number taken the West Coast between 1500 and 1850, primarily by European slave traders (~11,000,000), to get a total number of Africans shipped into slavery as somewhere in the vicinity of:

_____

Pic 66: Where are these Africans headed in chains and yokes?

_____

How many in the picture are driving them there, and with what kinds of weapons?

Pic 67 (bot): On the slave ship, of the slaves transported on the lower deck, how many were either children or Pygmies stored together?

_____

Why do you think people were placed by height?

_____

Royal African Company
_____

Middle Passage
_____

Slave Codes
_____

Quote 69: What argument did the Mennonites of Germantown, PA make against slavery?

Pic 69: Rice cultivation thrives most under

   a. wet conditions   *b. dry conditions*

_____

Pic 70: The city pictured is _____, from which exports of rice etc. left for England.

At right, draw a triangle with horizontal lines and label the class structure in places like this in and around the Colonial South.

_____

Pic 71: New England women had an amazing average of _____ children.

   a. six   *b. eight*   *c. ten*

of whom an average of _____ survived.

What were the divorce laws like in New England?

Quote 71: How did John White describe New England?

Quote 72: What does the Massachusetts School Law tell us about how the colonists regarded education?

The oldest college in America is:
|
|
|
|...founded in the year _____
|

Pic 73: Like the colonial school children, copy into this space the lessons learned while learning the ABCs:

A)   B)

C)   D)

E)   F)

G)   *As runs the glass, our life doth pass.*   *The rest are online if you search 'In Adam's Fall we sinned all'*

Congregational Church _____

Jeremiad _____

Half-Way Covenant _____

The Elect _____

Salem Witch Trials _____

Pic 74: If you were an elderly woman in 17th century England and you saw this dude roll up, you should probably

    a. answer the door   b. run

What did the New Englanders believe should be done with the land that they criticized the Indians for not doing?
|
|
|

Pic 75: Prudence Punderson's painting packed a plethora of powerful pictures into a poignant progression of a person's puttering through past, present and postmortem.

What did the combination of "Calvinism, soil and climate" in New England help encourage in the people?

| How did New England affect the rest
| of the nation's future philosophy?
|
|
|

Leisler's Rebellion _____

Why don't Dukes emigrate?

"So, there is this shipment of tea due in from India soon, want to…"

Quote 78: To Sam Adams, what did America allow for that others places in the world didn't?

_____

Of all Britain's _____ colonies in the America's, this many would join to rebel:

|

|

What does the term 'conquest by the cradle' mean and why were the English, like Dr. Johnson, perturbed by it?

| Which (European) races arrived and
| 'mingled' with the English at this point?
|
|
|
|

Map 79: This group especially used the 'great wagon road' to move into the Appalachian backcountry:

| This group moved especially into Pennsylvania:
|
| This group remained dominant up the Hudson River
| from New York City:
|

Chart 80: The first U.S. Census taken was in 1790. Replicate the bar graph below

	10%	20%	30%	40%	50%
English					
African					
Scottish					
German					
Scots-Irish					
Irish					
Dutch					
Other Euro					

Proportionally, the English majority had been　*a. rising*　*b. falling*　since the Pilgrims arrived.

Quote 80: What new 'race' did this French writer argue was being created? _____

Paxton Boys _____

Regulator Movement _____

As the slave population began including more women from Africa, the proportion of blacks who were born in Africa and transported versus those born in America

　a. grew　　*b. declined*　　*c. stayed the same*

| Some African words in the English
| language today are:
|
|
|
|

New York Slave Revolt

Contending Voices 81 – What were some attitudes about race described by the following:

Samuel Sewall – critic of slavery   *Virginia Slave Code – pro slavery*

Did these entities share any attitudes in common?

South Carolina Slave Revolt

Pg. 82: What are some of the things Africans did to become 'Makers of America'?

_____

_____

_____

If you've read the *Scarlet Letter*, you know Hester Prynne had to wear a large letter *A* for 'adulteress' because she became pregnant while her husband was lost at sea. On Pg. 84 we learn what big red letter had to be worn if a person was receiving charity from the taxpaying pubic.

What letter was it? | Today, nearly half of all Americans are on some from of public assistance
(use a nice red crayon or marker if handy) | Would you advocate these people wear a similar badge? Why or why not?

Pic 84: Of which positive features about the new shipment of slaves does this ad boast? | Why did the colonies try to stop slave imports?
|
| How did the British authorities react?
|

Quote 85: Why was Cotton Mather angry at Bostonians? | Do some people today still reject
| what the Bostonians back then
| were rejecting?

Out of clerics, physicians and lawyers (jurists), which job was least respected?

_____

Pic 86: The mighty catch was of _____.
The special location off the coast off Cape Cod where the fish were plentiful is called:

_____

Have you ever had cod? Is it good?

| Map 86: Note the economic activities of the following:

| Boston:

| New York:

| Philadelphia:

| Baltimore

| Norfolk:

| Charleston:

Triangular trade

Map 87: Complete the items transported by triangle trade for the following empires, inc. arrows:

	England			Spain / Portugal
English Colonies		Latin America		
	West Africa			West Africa

Molasses Act

Road conditions in America were generally

   a. surprisingly good   *b. really bad*

Pic 88: How are the tree and sun symbolic?

While big news can spread from Philadelphia to Charleston in less than 1 second today with an email or text, Charleston residents didn't know about the Declaration of Independence until a

| *a. day later*   *b. week later*   *c. month later*

Table 89 (bottom): Note the various denominations and their adherents on the eve of revolution:

Quote 90: What did Ben Franklin mean when he said, "A good example is the best sermon?"

What did he mean when he noted that, "Many quarrel about religion that never practiced it"?

Arminianism

The Great Awakening

Jonathan Edwards

George Whitefield

'Old lights', 'new lights'

Pic 91: Describe a George Whitefield sermon:

Quote 91: In Edwards' sermon, how are you seen by God?

Some 'new light' colleges that appeared were:

Pic 92: The look of Princeton when it first opened can be best described as:

a. lush and endowed   *b. austere and spartan*

What do you think the ABCs verse means?

Table 93: Note the nine colleges founded in colonial times and their location and year established

1

2

3

4

5

6

7

8

9

Pic 93: What is the use of this decorated item?

Quote 93: Of the seventeen subjects John Adams mentions he or his sons or grandsons will or may study, order them by how interesting they seem to you:

| Adams implies his sons and grandsons will study the things they want because

| a. they will be genetically enhanced

| b. by studying politics and war, Adams will help bring into existence a world in which his children will be able to live free and study what they want

Pic 94: Thanks to Ben Franklin's experiments with key and kite, the people shown here are beginning to understand and unlock the secrets of:

_____

Poor Richard's Almanack

In the Almanack shone Franklin's wisdom, but what do you think the statements meant?

SAYING   MEANING

"What maintains one vice would bring up two children"

"Plough deep while sluggards sleep"

"Honesty is the best policy"

"Fish and visitors stink in three days"

Zenger Trial

Royal colonies

Proprietary colonies

Why did backcountry people's resentment of coastal elites increase in the late colonial era?

| To what extent do you think backcountry Americans still resent political elites today?

Pic 96: What was the functional purpose of the gear the hunters of early America wore?

_____

Colonial assemblies

| Pic 97: Today there are tens of thousands of pool halls all across America, and people have billiard tables in their basements and game rooms all across the land. Where did this game come from? | Note the status in colonial America of the following:

home heating:

running water:

garbage disposal: |

Describe how different colonial life was from ours today regarding the following:

Item	*Then*	*Now*
Amusements		
Winter sports		
Lotteries		
Holidays		

Varying Viewpoints 98: What did the following historians have to say about colonial society?

Early Historians	*Richard Bushman*	*Gary Nash*
Christine Heyrman	*Jack Greene*	*Edmund S. Morgan*

Which of these do you agree with most?

Give a quick couple-word review of the following people:

John Trumbull	*John Singleton Copley*	*Phillis Wheatley*

Quote 101: The 'torch' lit sparked the Seven Years' War in Europe, the North American part of which was called the French and Indian War. But what do you think 'lit' the torch?

        a. territorial competition   *b. economic concerns*   *c. both of these*

Huguenots _____

St. Bartholomew's Day _____

Edict of Nantes _____

Louis XIV _____

St. Lawrence River _____

Quebec _____

Samuel de Champlain _____

'Lightning sticks' _____

Coureurs de bois _____

Voyageurs _____

Antoine Cadillac _____

Robert de La Salle _____

Map 102: Place the three competing empires in order of how much land they controlled in North America (Amerique du Nord, America del Norte) in 1700:

_____

Map 103: Note the operators of the fur-trading posts along the following waterways:

Mississippi: *St. Lawrence:*

Lake Huron: *Hudson Bay:*

Snake-Columbia: *Missouri:*

King William's War _____

Queen Anne's War _____

Table 104: Recall earlier we listed the Tudor and Stuart monarchs, now let's add to those lists the later monarchs of the colonial era:

Monarch   *Relation to America*

Map 104: Describe the fate of Schenectady, NY on the _____ River and Deerfield, MA during the war:

Treaty of Utrecht

War of Jenkin's Ear

King George's War

Pic 106: Why were the colonists angered after the war about the fate of Louisbourg?

Fort Duquesne

George Washington
(do NOT put something like "First President of the USA"... identify his significance in this chapter!)

Fort Necessity

Acadians (Cajuns)

French and Indian War

Seven Years' War

Map 108: During the Seven Year's 'Global' War, the first and last fighting took place on this continent:

How many battles took place in Dutch territory (Netherlands)?

Pic 109: What is the meaning behind Benjamin Franklin's famous *'Don't Tread on Me'* symbol inscribed with *'Join, or Die,'* later adapted for the Gadsden Flag?

Albany Congress _____

Edward Braddock _____

Regulars _____

'Buckskins' _____

In the Braddock drive west, who had two horses shot out from under him and four bullets go through his coat?	What happened to Braddock and the expedition?	How did the Indians celebrate this victory?

William Pitt _____

James Wolfe _____

Marquis de Montcalm _____

Battle of Quebec _____

Pic 110: Since the British and Scottish Act of Union (1707), the British identity had formed and the country was called Great Britain officially. It also flew a new flag, seen here, called The Union Jack. Draw and shade in the flag if you can, at right:

Note the territorial changes after the French and Indian War regarding the following:

French authority in North America   _France to Spain_   _Spain to Britain_

Map 111: These two rivers became the boundary between British and Spanish America:	Describe the location of Russia's holdings:

Pic 112: Fort 'Deh-twah' fell to Britain, how did that matter later?	"America was born on the Plaines d'Abraham." What does this historical interpretation mean?

Chief Pontiac _____

Proclamation of 1763

Contending Voices 113 - Summarize the statements of the following:

Proclamation of 1763   *George Washington*

Do you think the colonists justified in their resentment? Why?

Map 114: Sketch the red Proclamation Line of 1763 and a rough draft of the boundaries, rivers and cities east of the Mississippi:

Finally, go back to Map 107 and pinpoint the battles, using different symbols for British and French victories. Or, if you have colored pencils, use those. Good job!

From now on you have to pay a quarter for each sheet of paper your teacher gives you. Liking that Stamp Act yet?

Quote 117: According to John Adams, was the American Revolution was more than the war itself. What did he mean?

_____

Republicanism
_____

Radical Whigs
_____

Pic 118: What is "Lady Britain" saying to "Lady America?"   What does she say in response?

_____

Mercantilism
_____

What did the British do concerning the following that agitated the colonists?

Currency restrictions	*Nullification rights*	*Mercantilist system*

Navigation Laws
_____

Pic 119: Copley's painting of Revere shows: How is the theme of Franklin's quote similar?

_____

Sugar Act
_____

George Grenville
_____

Quartering Act
_____

Stamp Act

Admiralty courts

'Guilty until proven innocent'

'No taxation without representation'

Quote 120: What did Edmund Burke tell the young man to expect from America?	What distinction did Americans make between taxation and legislation?

Stamp Act Congress

Nonimportation agreements

Sons of Liberty

Daughters of Liberty

Pic 121: Sometimes an uproar comes around when people who buy American flags for the Fourth of July or some other holiday look and see their flag was made in China. How is this picture similar when we think about why the Chinese made those American flags?

Contending Voices 121 - Summarize the views of the following:

John Dickinson	Thomas Paine

Why do you think Paine's advice won out?

Declaratory Act

Townshend Acts

Pic 122: Who is this guy, what is his job, and what the heck are they doing to him?

_____

Pic 123: Do either of these images paint the British in a favorable light?	How do they differ (aside from being 86 years apart)?

Boston Massacre

George III

Lord North

Committees of Correspondence

Pic 124: Some Sam Adams accomplishments:	Some Abigail Adams accomplishments:

Boston Tea Party

Pic 125: As the tea party threw over the tea, and more come to join, what kind of disguises did they wear?	Quote 126: Loyalists like Ann Hulton were getting nervous as revolutionary fervor picked up. What did the Loyalists want to see happen?

Intolerable Acts

Quebec Act

First Continental Congress

The Association

Lexington and Concord

Pic 127: What were the largely Protestant Americans dismayed at the government for when they passed the Quebec Act	What was on the west side of the Appalachians?

Minute Men

Pic 128: The village green of Concord saw the British drilling. Why were they always called the 'Redcoats?'

What was the 'shot heard round the world' in Emerson's poem?

Quote 128: Edmund Burke has long been a hero to conservatives. What did he want to see happen?

Note the strengths and weaknesses of the imperial British forces and the American forces:

	Strengths	Weaknesses
British		
American		

*Thinking Globally 130 – How does this article **compare** the Tupac Amaru situation with the American?*

Marquis de Lafayette

Valley Forge

Camp followers

Lord Dunmore

Baron von Steuben

Don't start writing 'till you see the whites of the blanks where answers should be.

Quote 135: What do you think Thomas Paine meant by, "summer soldier and sunshine patriot?"

_____

_____

Second Continental Congress

The Congress wanted a 'redress of grievances' at this point, which best approximated:

a. giving up   *b. getting the government to make things right*   *c. full independence*

Note 10 character traits George Washington had that drove the Congress to give him command?

1	6
2	7
3	8
4	9
5	10

Pic 136: Who painted this famous painting of Washington? _____

Ethan Allen _____

Benedict Arnold _____

Capture of Fort Ticonderoga _____

Battle of Bunker Hill _____

Olive Branch Petition _____

Hessians _____

Pic 137: What do you think the caption means when it says Americans scored a 'moral victory' even though they had to abandon Bunker and Breed's Hill to the British?

_____

Assault on Quebec _____

Evacuation Day _____

Thomas Paine

Common Sense

Quote 139 (top): How does Paine feel about monarchy? | Pic 139: Does he *look* like he's *kidding*?

Quote 139 (bot.): According to Abbe Raynal, are America's principles for rebellious Englishmen alone, or for the oppressed of France as well? | What allusion did Paine make to the force of gravity in his writing?

Map 138: Note the dates of the following battles and maneuvers:

_____ *Lexington & Concord*   _____ *Long Island*   _____ *Fort Stanwix*

_____ *Battle of Bunker Hill*   _____ *Washington's Retreat*   _____ *Ft. Oriskany*

_____ *Siege of Boston*   <u>12/25/76</u> ***The Crossing***   _____ *Brandywine*

_____ *Lake Champlain*   _____ *Battle of Trenton*   _____ *Germantown*

_____ *Attack on Quebec*   _____ *Battle of Princeton*   _____ *Monmouth C.H.*

'Virtue'

Paine's pamphlet got people thinking about a republican form of government, but there was disagreement on whether 'the People' in general, had the civic virtue to make it work. Why do you think civic virtue is necessary in a system like ours? | What did the people who wanted 'natural aristocracy' argue for?

What did delegate Richard Henry Lee, ancestor of Civil War general Robert E. Lee, resolve at the Congress on June 7, 1776, which was adopted on July 2?

Declaration of Independence

Thomas Jefferson

Some of the complaints about the king included:

What similarities are there between Ben Franklin's quote: *"We must all hang together, or we will all hang separately,"* and the statement from the Declaration of Independence: *"We mutually pledge to each other our lives, our fortunes and our sacred honor"*:

_____

July 4, 1776
_____

Declaration of the Rights of Man
_____

Pic 141: What has modern science told us about King George III?

_____

Loyalists
_____

Patriots
_____

Pg. 142: Examining the Evidence. What about American history does this item illuminate?

_____

_____

_____

Patrick Henry
_____

How did the colonist rebels reflect the "Anglo-Saxon regard for order" in their treatment of Loyalists?

_____

Battle of Long Island
_____

William Howe
_____

Pg. 144: What are some of the things the Loyalists did to become 'Makers of America'?

_____

_____

_____

Battle of Trenton
_____

Pic 146: The story of a statue. Note the major events in the bio of this statue:

1766 – Put on a pedestal to honor the king, who:

1776 – Torn down to make _____ to use on the king's men.

Pic 147: Why was 'The Crossing' of the _____ River instrumental in boosting the Patriot's morale?

Gentleman John Burgoyne

Barry St. Leger

How did Benedict Arnold, whose name is synonymous in America with 'traitor,' due to later defection, get the British to do to win an essential strategic victory with his heroics on the lake?

Battle of Saratoga

Horatio Gates

Quote 148: Countries have often used diplomatic recognition as a way to influence and legitimize a new socio-political situation. In 2008, Serbia and Russia were angry when the United States and some others 'recognized' the new state of Kosovo, carved out of Serbia by Albanian migrants who settled there and declared independence. Put another way, if, say, California declared independence from the United States and Mexico and Canada quickly 'recognized' it as a country, it might lead to tension between them and the U.S. How does this quote mirror those situations?

Novus ordo seculorum

Model Treaty

Pic 149: 'America' was not just to be a country, but a new attitude. How did Ben Franklin use dress to demonstrate what that would be to the Europeans?

| What did Franklin do to set a precedent that "practical self-interest" would sometimes trump "abstract idealism?"

Armed Neutrality

Battle of Monmouth

Table 150: These countries joined in the war against Britain:

Comte de Rochambeau

How much did the British pay Benedict Arnold to sell out the fort of West Point and go traitor?	At this point, which part of the colonies did the British focus on to 'roll them up' and win?

Battle of King's Mountain

Battle of Cowpens

Nathanial Greene

Charles Cornwallis

Map 151: Lord Cornwallis arrived in Charleston by sea on this date: _____.

He then fought at King's Mountain and Cowpens and arrived in the coastal city: _____.

He then moved north in May 1781 to the emerging state of _____.

These two opponents met Cornwallis at Yorktown _____ & _____.

"Hair buyers"

The "Bloody Year"

Pic 152: Who did Joseph Brant, chief of the _____, side with? _____

Treaty of Ft. Stanwix

George Rogers Clark

Map 152: label the places significant during the George Rogers Clark campaign & the Ohio River:

*

*   *

*

Privateers

Quote 152: How were American soldiers 'different,' according to Baron von Stuben?

Pic 153: Describe the importance of the Battle of the Chesapeake Capes:

Admiral de Grasse

Battle of Yorktown

'The World Turn'd Upside Down'

'No Quarter for the Tories!'

Contending Voices 154 – What did the following say about how the American Revolution was different than the French Revolution, which began 8 years after Yorktown?

Friedrich von Gentz

John Quincy Adams

Note what the following desired at the time of the Treaty of Paris in 1783:

Spain

France

American delegates

Pic 155: What is going on in this cartoon?

Varying Viewpoints 156: What did the following historians have to say about the revolution?

George Bancroft

Beer/Andrews/Gipson

Carl Becker/J.F. Jameson

R. Brown/E. Morgan

Bernard Bailyn

Gary Nash

Woody Holton

Fred Anderson

David Armitage

Pg. 160   **9 – CONFEDERATION AND CONSTITUTION**   **Delegate** _____

People have the right to have rights. I think.

Quote 160: What does Jefferson believe America can provide a good example of to the world?

_____

The longest-lived constitution in the world is that of the State of	In the British tradition, a 'constitution' was not written, rather, it was:
_____	_____

Articles of Confederation
_____

Pg. 162: Examining the Evidence. What about American history does this item illuminate?

_____

_____

_____

Pic 163: Who are these merchants and what are they doing in this picture?

_____

The Articles of Confederation focused on the   *legislative*   *executive*   *judicial*   branch.

_____

Map 164: What did it mean for a state to 'cede land to the United States?'	Pic 165: Note some of the historic events that took place at Independence Hall, Philadelphia:

Highlight some of the 'weaknesses' of the Articles of Confederation that prompted the founders to think about replacing it:

Old Northwest
_____

Land Ordinance of 1785

Northwest Ordinance

Map 166: Draw a township (left) and a square mile division under L.O. of 1785:

Note how Britain acted against American economic interests in these years- mention Lord Sheffield:	Note how Spain acted against American economic interests in these years:

Map 167: The centers of British and Spanish power in U.S. territory were:

    British   *Spanish*

John Jay

Shays' Rebellion

Pic 168: How did the presence of so many people in debt affect national leaders?

Constitutional Convention

'Sword of the Revolution'

'The elder statesman'

'Father of the Constitution'

Alexander Hamilton

Dey of Algiers

Pic 170: Franklin commented on the symbolism of Washington's tall chair. What did he mean?	Describe the characteristics of the 55 legislators

Virginia Plan

New Jersey Plan

The Great Compromise

House of Representatives

Senate

Common law

Civil law

Electoral College

Three-fifths Compromise

Checks and balances

"We the People"

Pic 172: How long in total hours spent did the Constitution take to draft in 1787? _____

Table 173: What did the Constitution have to say about the following:

Importing more slaves   *Runaway slaves*

Quote 173: What do you think Ben Franklin was implying in his famous answer to the woman who asked him about the kind of government America was to have?

Antifederalists

Federalists

Table 174: In what ways was the Constitution stronger than the Articles of Confederation?

Map 175: Generalize the location of people who were more antifederalist in their beliefs:

Table 175: Why do you think Delaware calls itself "the First State?"

The Federalist

Pic 176: The Society of Pewterers is most like   *a modern cartel*   *a medieval guild*

Pic 177: Draw
and label the
pillars:

The final document is best described as: *radical*   *conservative*   *monarchical*

Contending Voices 177 – What did the following argue concerning the Constitution:

   Jonathan Smith   *Patrick Henry*

Who do you agree with more?

Society of the Cincinnati

Disestablishment

Pic 178: Americans love forming groups and societies. What was the point of this one?

_____

_____

Virginia Statute for Religious Freedom
_____

Quote 179: Analyze both the quotes on this page:

Top   Bottom

Who said it:

What did they say:

When did they say it:

Where did they say it:

Why did they say it:

_____

Civic virtue
_____

Republican motherhood
_____

Pic 179: What did Elizabeth Mumbet Freeman do?	How is it similar to what the Africans on the island in the quote thought?

Varying Viewpoints 180: How did each historian argue?

John Fiske   *Charles A. Beard*   *Brown & McDonald*

Gordon Wood   *David Waldstreicher*   *Woody Holton*

Federalist: "Everyone come to Washington D.C. for a meeting." Antifederalist: "Let's just Skype this meeting. Seriously. We don't need to go there."

Quote 182: Based on his quote here, do you think Alexander Hamilton would have advised President George W. Bush to go ahead with the plan to bring American-style democratic government to Iraq in 2003? Why or why not?

_____

The section entitled "Growing Pains" points out that the total population of the United States reached 4 million by 1790. What is the closest metropolitan area to you with a population of over 4 million?

Quote 182: Robert Turgot was France's top economist of the day. How did he regard the new experiment of America?

_____

_____

The only president to ever have been elected unanimously was _____

Of the long list of cabinet positions on pg. 183, list the ones that are still the same, and the ones that are gone or transformed:

The same   *Gone*

Bill of Rights _____

How do the following guarantee non-enumerated rights to remain with the states and the people:

Ninth Amendment   *Tenth Amendment*

Judiciary Act of 1789 _____

Pic 184: What does this poster say George Washington is? _____

_____

Funding at par

Assumption

Pic 185: Contrast Jefferson's vision of an ideal America with Hamilton's:

Jefferson   *Hamilton*

Chart 186: How much total debt did the USA have during this time? _____

Tariff

Do the authors of the textbook seem pro-Hamilton or pro-Jefferson? Demonstrate your position using a quote from this section, which may be adjectives use to describe their respective doings:

Excise tax

Pic 187: How do you *know* the cartoonist favors the rebels who opposed Hamilton's tax?

Bank of the United States

Whiskey Rebellion

Quote 187: Which founder, Jefferson or Hamilton, had more confidence in the people of America to take care of themselves without control from above?

Quote 188: What did Breckenridge say about the Whiskey Rebel situation?

Is it strange they don't tell you, student and reader, that foreign interests owned much of the Bank of 'America?' Or that the 'Bank of America' was in fact a private corporation given the right to mint money, just like its descendent, the Federal Reserve Bank (the Fed), does today? If someone asked you to find evidence that the authors of the textbook are very pro-Hamilton and anti-Jefferson, could you find any such evidence on pg. 186?

Does the textbook laud or criticize the two-party system? _____

What do you think the authors of the textbook mean when they write, "The party out of power traditionally plays the invaluable role of the balance wheel on the machinery of government"?

Chart 189: Copy the chart to see how the parties currently in power were formed:

French Revolution

Pic 189: Why were some Americans disgusted with the French Revolution?

*Thinking Globally 190 – How does this article **compare** the French Revolution with the American?*

Reign of Terror

Neutrality Proclamation

Anthony Wayne

Battle of Fallen Timbers

Chief Little Turtle

Treaty of Greenville

Map 193: Which territories that would Become states in the future were added to the U.S. after 1783?

| Pic 194: What was the overall consequence of the U.S.-Indian conflicts during this era?

Quote 194: Was Paine's prophecy correct?   *Yes, definitely*   *No, not really*

Jay's Treaty

Pinckney's Treaty

Washington's Farewell Address

What did Washington recommend for the country in the Farewell Address?

Pic 195: Recalling his lucid defense of the Boston Massacre shooters in the British Army, what other pursuits did John Adams have before going for law?

Quote 196: Jefferson's statement indicates God is distant from human affairs. This Corresponds most with (see pg. 309):

Traditional Christianity   deism   atheism

Pic 196: What caused the XYZ Affair?

| The slogan raised against France at this
| time was:
|
|

Pic 197: The *Philadelphia* would see action in the battle against the Barbary Pirates. Look up what country the city of Tripoli, from which they came, is the capital of today:

Convention of 1800

Alien Laws

Sedition Act

Matthew Lyon

Pic 199: What exactly is going on in this picture and why is it happening?

Virginia Resolution

Kentucky Resolution

What did John Jay think about who should govern the United States?

|

Copy Table 200 to see the contrast in the political platforms of the following parties:

The Federalists   *The Democratic-Republicans*

1.

2.

3.

4.

5.

6.

7.

8.

9.

10.

11.

12.

13.

_____

Pic 201: What did it mean that Jefferson was a "natural bridge?"

_____

Quote 201: What does Jefferson say he wants in this statement?

_____

_____

_____

So you agree with the Jeffersonian vision of America? Why or why not?

_____

Teacher: "From now on there's going to be a property requirement for you to turn in late work." Students: "Huh?"

Quote 204: What do the following mean in Jefferson's statement and beyond:

Despotism   *Boisterous*   *Mudslinging*

_____   _____   _____

Note some of the fire the Federalists came under during this era:

_____

"Whispering campaign"

Quote 204: In France at the time, Jacobin (radicals) were tearing down old Gothic churches and putting up 'temples of wisdom' in their place. When the Rev. Timothy Dwight says American sons will be converted to Voltaire and Marat, he means they will lose religion and become

a. too liberal   b. too moderate   c. too conservative

Pic 205: What is this propaganda ad trying to get people to think about?

_____

_____

_____

Lame Duck

Revolution of 1800

Map 206: Geographically speaking, where were the states that voted against Jefferson located?

Quote 206: Why was this lady so amazed at the way U.S. administration ran?

Pg. 207: Examining the Evidence. The first American presidential sex-scandal!

If you were a lawyer trying to accuse Jefferson of being the father of at least some of Sally Hemmings' children, what evidence would you present from this article?

_____

_____

_____

| Hmm... interesting. Now take note:
| 1 – DNA results say a male in the
| Jefferson line was the father of one
| of Sally's many children- Eston. But
| there were 26 male Jeffersons with that
| DNA around her at the time.
|
| 2 – Sally was 14 and accompanied
| Jefferson in Paris as a maid, along with
| his daughters of the same age. Seriously?
| Jefferson was 64 at the time. The
| daughters both denied it too. Now what?
|

Pic 208: The carriage at the foot of the daughter in this picture is said to be attesting to her:

      a. poverty- it was the only one they had   *b. wealth and privilege*

Did you have any toys like that-
 cars etc. when you were a kid?

     a. yes   *b. no*

If there were no cameras all over with people taking
pics- selfies and otherwise- and you only had one
shot at a family portrait, what would you wear:

     a. regular clothes   *b. your best clothes*

Pic 209: What kind of clothes did Jefferson favor?

_____

Quote 209: What was Kennedy's opinion of T.J.?

We know the polygraph as a lie-detector
machine. But what did Jefferson use this
one for?

_____

Judiciary Act of 1801

"Midnight Judges"

John Marshall

Marbury v. Madison

Pic 211: John Marshall was   *a. born into wealth*   *b. a rags-to-riches story*

Jefferson was a war hawk, ready to entangle in international alliances: *a. true*   *b. false*

Barbary states

The pashas of North Africa organized the pirates,
agents of Muslim states based in these cities:

_____

Map 212: Where did the major battle take place?

_____

Their 'piracy' was raiding the Spanish, Italian
and other coasts looking for villagers to capture
as slaves, and extortion. How did Jefferson
respond to these states' demands for tribute?

_____

Pic 212: Why did the Americans burn their own ship, the *Philadelphia,* as shown here?

Note the results of the Tripolitan War and how it affect the U.S. military and psyche:

Explain the situation in France when Napoleon agreed to sell the Louisiana Territory:

Haitian Revolution

Pic 214: Toussaint led the ex-slaves in the French colony of Saint-Domingue (Haiti) against the French, and killed many before Napoleon had him captured and brought to France. What happened to him then?

What happened to the colony?

Louisiana Purchase

Corps of Discovery

Lewis & Clark

Sacajawea

Zebulon Pike

Pic 215: Describe the journey of Lewis and Clark:

Pic 216 (left): Why did Clark refer to these Indians as 'flatheads?'

Pic 216 (right): What might be the propaganda value of giving the Indian chiefs of the west these medallions?

Map 217: Along the border of which modern states did Lewis & Clark find the Pacific?

Aaron Burr

Why do the authors refer to Britain and France as the 'Tiger and the Shark' in this period?

Orders in Council

Impressment

Chesapeake Affair

Embargo Act of 1807

Pic 219: Why do you think people who live in coastal towns tend to be against embargos?

Contending Voices 219 – Why the different perspectives

Non-Intercourse Act

Quote 220: What utterly amazing coincidence occurred on July 4, 1826?

Pic 221: What are the British and French shown doing here?

Macon's Bill #2

Did Madison's gamble work? Why or why not?

Tecumseh

War Hawks

Pic 222: Note the consequences of the battles of the Themes and Tippecanoe:

William Henry Harrison

"Scalp buyers"

Quote 222: Henry Clay was most definitely

    a. a hawk   *b. a dove*

Quote 222 (right): Is Tecumseh a capitalist?

    a. totally   *b. yeah right*

Pic 223: Note the political positions of the following during this time:

    Jeffersonians   *Federalists*

In closing, if you could go back in time and talk to Jefferson, would you advise him to purchase Louisiana? Why?

"You may have to water the tree of liberty every 20 years or so." With what? "Oh nothing, just the blood of patriots and tyrants."

Quote 226: What was James Monroe's message to Europe and Asia in 1823?

_____

War of 1812

From which three places were American troops dispatched for Canada in 1812?

1   2   3

Rate the action of the American Navy in 1813 as against both the American Army and the British:

_____

"Old Ironsides"

Oliver Hazard Perry

Detroit is the only American city to have surrendered to a foreign force since the independence of the country. Who did it surrender to in the War of 1812?	Map 227: After which battle on Lake Erie did Perry say, "We have me the enemy and they are ours," reinvigorating the American cause?
Map 227: Which large U.S. city was burned to the ground by the British?	Map 227: Before the great Battle of New Orleans, maybe the most famous unnecessary battle in history, where did Jackson fight the Creek Indian Red Sticks?

Pic 228: What did Henry Adams say after the U.S.S. *Constitution* defeated the H.M.S. *Guerriere* at sea?

_____

Thomas Macdonough

Fort McHenry

Francis Scott Key

Star Spangled Banner

The Battle of New Orleans happened   *a. before*   *b. after*   the war was over.

(Whatever you do, don't Youtube: Battle of New Orleans Johnny Horton and listen to it on loudest volume in the middle of class)

Congress of Vienna

Treaty of Ghent

Quote 229: During the Haitian Revolution a decade earlier, white French soldiers caught malaria and the disease killed more of them than the enemy fighters. Ultimately, they had to withdraw because of it, and it was determined that Europeans should not fight in tropical climes during the summer malarial season. Jackson knew this. What evidence of that is here in this quote?

Pic 230: What kinds of things did the British promise to states willing to quit the Union and rejoin the British Empire?

Hartford Convention

Quote 231: What was this British lieutenant's opinion of Americans and American soldiers?

Map 231: In the 1812 election, generalize about the location of the states who voted for Clinton:

While the authors state (231) the War of 1812 was "but a footnote" to the Napoleonic Wars going on in Europe, what did the war do for Americans?

Rush-Bagot Agreement

Pic 232: What does 'rustic' mean in the context of this picture of the White House in 1826?

Tariff of 1816

The American System

Pic 233: What kinds of policies might the U.S. government enact today that would be like a modern version of the American System?

James Monroe

Era of Good Feelings

| Pic 234: Aside from Old Glory, what other distinctively American symbols are there here? | Quote 234: The message presented here is:

a. meant to be ironic   b. You are a lucky country America, enjoy while it lasts |

Panic of 1819

| Some causes of the Panic of 1819 were: | Pic 235: The mode of transportation for many pioneers was: |

Land Act of 1820

Tallmadge Amendment

The "Peculiar Institution"

Pic 236: Don't read the caption yet! If you saw these silk bags in a museum, with black women doing work and slaves being whipped, which of the following would you think it was at first sight?

a. racist, pro-slavery propaganda   b. abolitionist anti-slavery propaganda

Were you right after reading the caption?   a. yes   b. no

Missouri Compromise

| Map 237: What did the North get out of giving up Missouri to the South? | Quote(s) 237: What were the opinions of Jefferson and Adams on slavery and the race issue in America? |

Pg. 238: What are some of the things the Settlers of the Old Northwest did to become 'Makers of America'?

John Marshall

Pic 241: Webster's great quote was:

Note the judicial significance of the following cases:

McCulloch v. Maryland   *Cohens v. Virginia*

Gibbons v. Ogden   *Fletcher v. Peck*

Dartmouth v. Woodward   Quote 240: What was the chief criticism
                                           of John Marshall by the NY Times?

Oregon Country

Anglo-American Convention

Map 242: What year did the U.S.-British | Why do you think what is now Northern Maine was
Treaty Line decide the border between | disputed by the U.S. and Britain?
the U.S. and Canada? |
|
|
|
| (Whatever you do, do NOT do a video search for 'SNL Maine Justice' to see how it was settled)

Map 242 (bot.): Note Jackson's response to | After hanging the two British officials at St.
the Indian raids into Georgia and the | Marks and 'pacifying' the Indians and escaped
Mississippi Territory: | slaves in the interior of Florida, where did
| Jackson head next to encounter the Spanish?
|
|

Adams-Onis Treaty

Pic 243: What did people mean by giving | Why did many feel the world had to be made safe
Jackson the nickname "Old Hickory?" | *from* democracy after the French Revolution?
|
|
|

Russo-American Treaty

Pic 244: Compare the map on Monroe's wall | Quote 245: Why might the Colombian
in the background against the map on pg. 243. | newspaper be more positive about the *Monroe*
What is different about the two? | *Doctrine* than Metternich?
|
|

*"I... killed... the bank!" -President Andrew Jackson; his last words before he died, when asked about his **greatest** accomplishment.*

Quote 248: Under what conditions did Jackson argue American people had a right to complain about the injustice of their government?

Corrupt Bargain

Describe the political status of the following:

    John Q. Adams   *Henry Clay*

    John C. Calhoun   *Andrew Jackson*

Pic 249: What does it mean when it says politicians realized they had to "get the message to the man"?	Jackson was by far the most popular in 1824- why didn't he win?
Pic 250: J.Q. Adams was the first "Minority President"- what does the term mean?	Note some of the things Adams did that the public didn't like while in office:

When the nation went "Whole Hog" for Jackson in the mid-1820s after the Corrupt Bargain, what were some of the slogans they used? Which was the most catchy to you?

1   2   3

Map 252: Which candidate did Michigan, Arkansas and Florida vote for in 1828? (trick question)	Quotes 252: Contrast the three opinions of the polarizing Jackson *Anti-Jackson Newspaper* *Maryland Supporter* *Jefferson*

Quote 253: What did Charles Dickens (who wrote *A Christmas Carol* and *A Tale of Two Cities*) think about America's common-man equality?

_____

Spoils system

Thinking Globally 254: "Democracy in America" is one of the great works of American history, and a Frenchman wrote it! He came, he saw, he wrote about the U.S. in its youth. Note three distinctive things he described about the country:

1)   2)   3)

Tariff of Abominations

Protectionism

Quote 256: Why did John C. Calhoun use the term 'union' or 'confederacy' instead of 'nation' when describing the U.S.A.?

_____

Pic 256: South Carolina started the Civil War (at least- it helped trigger the beginning of hostilities) by seceding from the U.S. on December 26, 1860. How many years *before* this event did South Carolina begin *thinking* about seceding?	Pic 257: Calhoun believed in the Union, but what did he argue was necessary to preserve the Union?

The South Carolina Exposition

Nullification

Do you think a state should be able to nullify a federal law that the state believes is unconstitutional *or* not in its best interests? Why or why not?	Quote 257: Whose toast would you have cheered most- Jackson's or Calhoun's?

Compromise Tariff of 1833

Force Bill

Pic 258: Today forced separation of one people from another, such as white Americans and Indians, is called ethnic cleansing. What was Jackson's rationale for moving the tribes to reservations out west?

| Describe the steps the Cherokees took to assimilate to white American culture before being removed to reservations anyway:

Pic 259: Out of the fifteen thousand Cherokees that were ethnically cleansed by the U.S. Army, how many actually made it?

| Is ethnic cleansing going on in places in the world today?

        Y   N

(look it up if you don't know)

Indian Removal Act

Trail of Tears

Black Hawk War

Chief Oceola

Seminole War

Map 260: Name all the tribes that were moved west to Indian Territory:

| Pic 261: Is Black Hawk or his son more assimilated to American ways?

| _____

| Many U.S. sports teams are names after Indian-related themes. Chicago's hockey team is the Blackhawks, named for the chief shown here. Do you think this is offensive or does it do honor to the man?

Bank of the United States

What made 'The Bank' a 'moneyed monster' in Jackson's eyes?

| 'The Bank' was:

| *a. a government institution*
| *b. a private company*

Nicholas Biddle

The Bank War

How did Clay try to use 'The Bank' to surefire win the next election against Jackson?	How did Jackson shock the government in response?

Jackson was shot by an assassin but survived, and blamed international banking interests for hiring the killer. He called 'The Bank' a 'many-headed hydra' too, but even more seriously, what famous quote did he speak, notifying privately what he would do to 'The Bank' in return?

Pic 262: What are the following doing in this comic, and what does it mean?

> *The Pro-Bank Men*   *Biddle*   *Jackson*

Literally:

Meaning:

Quote 262: It is   *likely*   *unlikely*   that Biddle really was "delighted" with Jackson's veto.

Anti-Masonic party

On a 1-10 scale, how much credence do you give to conspiracy theories about the Illuminati, the Mason, the Rothschild bankers etc.?	Pic 263: What sly move does Jackson use to disarm Biddle in the fight for 'The Bank?'

Biddle's Panic

Pet banks

Specie Circular

Martin Van Buren

MVB was a man of many nicknames. Provide four of them, and judge whether it has a positive or negative connotation:

1   *3*

2   *4*

Pg. 265: Examining the Evidence. What about American history does this item illuminate?

_____

_____

Panic of 1837

Pic 266: Why didn't anyone relish getting a 'Long Bill'? | Quote 266: Why is a bank run a
                                                             | economically dangerous thing?
                                                             |
                                                             |
                                                             |
                                                             |

Davy Crockett

Jim Bowie

Sam Houston

Steve Austin

Note the development of events during the following years in Texas:

_1821:_   _1833:_

_1823:_   _1835:_

_1830:_   _1836:_

Pic 267: The leader and hero of the Texas rebels was   Pic 268: The message of the Texans was:

_____   _____

Santa Anna

Battle of the Alamo

Battle of Goliad

Battle of San Jacinto

Pic 268 (bot.): Why did the Alamo become a | Map 269: What was strategic about Houston's
rallying cry for the Texas and the Americans? | retreat toward the United States?
                                               |
                                               |
                                               |

Why do you think the Americans help the Texans at crucial moments during the Texas Revolution?

_____

Okay one last nickname for Martin van Buren: _____

Pg. 270: What are some of the things the Anglo 'Texicans' did to become 'Makers of America'?

_____

_____

_____

"Old Tippecanoe"

John Tyler

Pic 272: Why did Harrison and Tyler have these kerchiefs made for women- when women couldn't vote?	What role did log cabins and hard cider play in this election?

Pic 273: Explain what is happening to Van Buren:

On the Left   *On the Right*

Do you think all presidents go through something like this? Why or why not?

Two-Party System

Relate the status of the two national parties after 1840:

The Democrats (Differences)	Similarities	The Whigs (Differences)

Pic 274: Is this painting a good reflection on the age? Why or why not?

Quote 274: Jackson's advice as to how to know a Democrat from a Whig said one should...

Pg. 275: Varying Viewpoints. What did the following historians have to say about Jacksonian democracy?

Frederick Jackson Turner	*Arthur Schlesinger*	*Richard Hofstadter*
Marvin Meyers	*Lee Benson*	*Sean Wilentz*
Charles Sellers	*Daniel Walker How*	Which do you agree with most?

Quote 278: Emerson believes the advancement of new technologies | Emerson also believes

a. *bolsters established governments*   b. *diffuses central power* | a. *America is stodgy & old*

The American West was   a. *tough*   b. *full of opportunities*   c. *both* | b. *America is vital & new*

Self-reliance _____

Rendezvous _____

Ecological imperialism _____

Map 279: Note the year the center of American population passed the following cities:

_____ *Washington, D.C.*   _____ *Pittsburgh, PA*   _____ *Cleveland, OH*

_____ *Cincinnati, OH*   _____ *Chicago, IL*   _____ *St. Louis, MO*

Pic 280: What evidence do we have here that European noblemen were fascinated with the rugged American West? | What evidence do we have that the West was sometimes a little too rugged?

Note some big-city problems that appeared due to rapid urbanization in the mid-19th century:

Graph 281: Describe the general pattern of growth by race leading up to 1860: | Alright math nerds, figure this one out. Given that during the Civil War in the 1860s a total of 580,000 whites died and 40,000 nonwhites, did the trend continue in *that* decade? Show your work ;)

_____

_____

_____

_____

Graph 281 (bot.):   *Which decade did the most Irish people immigrate to America?* _____

          Which decade did the most German people immigrate to America? _____

Quote 281: Describe two kinds of people coming to America from Germany in the 19th century:

_____

Pic 282: The 19th century's equivalent of widescreen TV, describe the uniquely American reasons artists chose the aesthetic shown here:

_____

There were more Irish-Americans by the end of the 19th century than there were Irish: *T   F*

Ancient Order of Hibernians _____

Molly Maguires _____

Tammany Hall _____

Quote 283: What kind of advice did Margaret McCarthy write to her relatives in Ireland?	Quote 283: The French writer was shocked that
	a. Indians and blacks had it bad in America
	b. In Ireland things were even worse c. Both

48ers _____

Kindergarten _____

Pg. 285: What are some of the things the Irish did to become 'Makers of America'?

_____

_____

_____

Pic 286: This cartoon implies two things about the Irish and Germans. What are they?

1)   2)

_____

Know-Nothing party _____

Awful Disclosures _____

Nativists _____

Industrial Revolution _____

Quote 287: The Know-Nothing platform said:	Transcendentalist Orestes Brownson said:

Samuel Slater _____

Textiles _____

Eli Whitney _____

Cotton gin _____

Pg. 288: What are some of the things the Germans did to become 'Makers of America'?

_____

_____

_____

| Pic 290: What did this factory mill produce? | Describe the rise and fall of the early mills between the years 1807 and 1816: |

Samuel Colt _____

Patent Office _____

Pic 291: How did the cotton gin affect plantation life and slavery as a labor system?

_____

_____

Limited liability _____

Samuel Morse _____

Charles Goodyear _____

Quote 292: _____ remains the only president ever to have obtained a patent.

Quote 292 (bot.): Describe conditions for factory workers in New England:

Besides European indentured servants and African slaves, companies used white kids to do these kinds of jobs:

'Scabs' and 'rats'

Commonwealth v. Hunt

Quote 293: What does the term 'trade union' mean in this statement?

_____

Pic 293: Which job would you rather have, the one on the right or the left? Why?

_____

Pg. 294: Examining the Evidence. What about American history does this item illuminate?

_____

_____

Factory girls

Cult of domesticity

Pic 295: Would you have rather been a girl who worked in a factory or mill as in this picture, or have been a homemaker? Why?

_____

Pic 296: How do you know the black woman in this picture is employed by the household and not a slave?	Where was McCormick's factory located?

McCormick reaper

Pic 298: What do you think was the general level of sound working at this factory? _____

Turnpike

Robert Fulton

Clermont

Pic 299: Would you have rather been a passenger on one of the boats pictured or on the *Sultana*? Why?

_____

Erie Canal

The Iron Horse

Map 300: In order to get by boat from New York City to Detroit, one can take the

_____
to Albany, followed by the

_____
to Buffalo, followed by

_____
to Detroit.

'Sleeping Palace'
_____

George Pullman
_____

Clipper ships
_____

One could get from Chicago to Indianapolis by road in this era:

    a. True   *b. False*

It was possible to get from New York City to New Orleans by boat stopping at Chicago on the way:

    a. True   *b. False*

Map 301: The densest area of the country for railroad lines was:

    a. the industrial north   *b. the agrarian south*

Map 303: Before the Civil War, the Pony Express carried mail from Salt Lake City to San Francisco:

a. True   *b. False*

Mark Twain implied the coach trip to California was very:

a. mountainous and difficult   *b. easy*

Pony Express
_____

Transportation revolution
_____

Market revolution
_____

Describe how the economic climate changed under Chief Justice Roger Taney:

_____

Map 305: Note the states that specialized in the following:

Flour mills:

Textile mills:

Shoes/clothes:

Iron and steel:

_____

Map 305: Note the states that had the following resources:

Silver and gold:

Copper:

Iron:

Coal:

Map 305: Note the states that specialized in the following agricultural products:

Corn and wheat: *Dairy and hay:*

Tobacco and hemp: *Cotton, rice and sugarcane:*

Map 305: Note the states that specialized in the following products:

Range and ranch cattle:

Orchard fruits:

Lumber and timber:

John Jacob Astor

'Drifters'

'Rags to riches' story

Pic 306: Chicago was laid out in a   *a. regular grid*   *b. irregular natural*   pattern.

Timeline 307: What kind of invention did John Deere have before getting into the tractor business?	Under President Van Buren, federal workers began working this many hours:

London's great fair that displayed all the new inventions of the age was held in _____

What did Howe and Singer invent?	What did Cyrus Field accomplish?

No, you are not allowed to Missouri Compromise your way out of doing half this assignment.

Quote 309: This Emerson quote is about: *a. growing up*   *b. America*   *c. both*

The Age of Reason

Deism

After examining the Tocqueville quote and the bases of deism, summarize how America's religiosity was changing in the mid-19th century:

_____

_____

Second Great Awakening

Pic 310: How is a revival such as this one different than a traditional church service?	Pic 311: Name three things Charles Finney argued would help bring society closer to recreating God's heavenly kingdom on earth:

Burned-Over District

Joseph Smith

Mormons

Pic 312: The Mormon trek west is most like the video game: *a. Oregon Trail* *b. Minesweeper* *c. GTA VI*	Map 313: The Mormons followed this natural feature much of the way to Utah:

Brigham Young

Quote 313: What is polygamy, as it is referred to in this statement?	What years did Congress pass anti-polygamy laws?

Pic 314: If you were a lawyer arguing both sides of this question, what would your main arguments be?

Public education like this schoolhouse is free   *Public education is not really free*

Complete the famous Thomas Jefferson quote:

"A civilized nation that was both ignorant and free...   *"*

Horace Mann _____

Noah Webster _____

William McGuffey _____

Emma Willard _____

Quote 315: After reading the two quote about education on this page, first by Lincoln and next by Sarah Hale, argue whether they agree or disagree and why:	Pic 316: How had opportunities for women in higher education changed between 1837 and 1872?

Lyceum _____

Godey's Lady's Book _____

Quote 316: What did Dorothea Dix find troubling about the way the mentally ill were being treated?	Pic 317: What did Ms. Dix argue would be a better way to treat people in jail?

Pic 318: Note some of the negative things happening in America due to heavy drinking:

_____

American Temperance Society _____

Ten Nights in a Barroom _____

Maine Law _____

Pic 319: If you were a lawyer arguing both sides of this question, what would your main arguments be?

        Women have it pretty good   *Women are the 'Submerged sex'*

Elizabeth Cady Stanton

Susan B. Anthony

| Pic 320: Do you agree with the statement that this image doesn't seem absurd today? Why or why not? | Quote 320: What do these wedding vows mean in layman's (or layperson's) terms? |

Seneca Falls

Pg. 321: Examining the Evidence. How can clothes be a symbol of social reform?

_____

_____

_____

New Harmony

Brook Farm

Oneida Community

Shakers

If you could go back in time, which of these four communities would you most want to join?

_____

Contending Voices 322 - Summarize the views of the following:

    Seneca Falls writer   *Reform newspaper*

With whom do you agree more?

Pic 323 (top): The Shakers are best described as: *a. hard working*   *b. lazy*

Note the achievements of the following American scientists:

Nathanial Bowditch   *Matthew Maury*   *Benjamin Silliman*

Louis Agassiz   *Asa Gray*   *John Audubon*

Pg. 324: What are some of the things the Oneidans did to become 'Makers of America'?

_____

_____

_____

Some nasty medical conditions people complained about in the mid-19th century (before the germ theory of disease gained prevalence) were:	Name three common remedies practiced back then that you would totally not use: 1 2 3

Federal style _____

Greek-Revival _____

Monticello _____

Pic 327: Thomas Jefferson's favorite style to design buildings in was _____

Note the kind of art produced by the following:

Gilbert Stuart   *Charles W. Peale*   *John Trumbull*

Hudson River School _____

Thomas Cole _____

Albert Bierstadt _____

Louis Daguerre

Minstrel shows

What would your English teacher say is ironic about the origin of the famous Southern songs *Dixie, Camptown Races, Old Folks at Home* and *Oh! Susanna*?	While the British made fun of American writing, these nonfiction books stood out:

Romanticism

Pic 328: What elements in this painting make it a masterpiece of the Romantic style?

Match the fiction writer with their famous works:

Washington Irving:

James Fennimore Cooper:

William Cullen Bryant:

Transcendentalism

What did the Transcendentalists believe?

Pic 330: If you had to read a book by one of the authors pictured here, who would it be?

The American Scholar

Note the contributions of the following Transcendentalist writers:

Ralph Waldo Emerson   *Henry David Thoreau*

Margaret Fuller   *Walt Whitman*

Quote 331: After reading both of these quotes, answer the question: "Henry David Thoreau would

a. argue you are a good citizen when you do what you are told and are nonviolent
b. argue you are a good citizen when you do what you think is right violently
c. argue you are a good citizen when you do what you are told and are violent about it
d. argue you are a good citizen when you do what you think is right and are nonviolent

Note the contributions of the following 'literary lights':

H.W. Longfellow   *John G. Whittier*

James Russell Lowell   *Louisa May Alcott*

Emily Dickinson   *William Gilmore Simms*

Note the contributions of the following 'dissenting' writers and 'portrayers of the past':

Edgar Allan Poe   *Nathanial Hawthorne*

Herman Melville   *George Bancroft*

William Prescott   *Francis Parkman*

What about these historians was suspect to Southerners?   Pic 334: Would you work in whaling?

Viewpoints 335: What did these historians argue about the 19ᵗʰ century women's movement?

Michael Katz   *B. Quarles & J.B. Stewart*   *Cott, Sklar & Ryan*

C.S. Rosenberg   *N. Hewitt & L. Ginzberg*   *Ellen DuBois*

Quote 340: Lincoln's warning seems to advocate:

a. ending slavery because it is in everyone's best interest   *b. denying freedom to all*

'King Cotton'
_____

Why could the Antebellum South be called a political oligarchy instead of a democracy? | Why did so many Southerners love the novels of Sir Walter Scott?

Pic 341: The cotton bales in this picture are in the city of

_____ headed for _____

What kinds of items manufactured in the North agitated many Southerners because it reminded them of dependence? | Pic 342: What are the slave workers doing in this picture?

_____

Graph 343: The fewest number of slaveowning families owned | The great majority of Southern whites owned _____ slaves.

_____ slaves, the most owned _____. | _____

This was not an insult that was applied to poor whites in the old South:

a. poor white trash   *b. ninjas*   *c. crackers*   *d. hillbillies*

Map 344: In general, the distribution of Southern cotton production between 1820 and 1860:

a. moved north by northwest   *b. moved west by southwest*   *c. did not move*

Map 345: This state did not have any counties containing over 50 percent slaves in 1860:

a. Georgia   *b. South Carolina*   *c. North Carolina*   *d. Virginia*   *e. Missouri*

William T. Johnson
_____

What kinds of social rules existed for the 'Third Race' of free blacks in the South?

Frederick Douglass
_____

West Africa Squadron

Pic 347: Most slaves caught in the Congo were sent to Brazil or the Caribbean, but what is the story of Solomon Northrup on the right?

| Why were Irish laborers more likely to be hired for dangerous jobs by Southern planters than having slaves undertake them?

Quote 348: Locate three grammar or spelling errors in this letter by Maria Perkins:

Uncle Tom's Cabin

Pic 348: Aside from the slaves being sold at the action depicted on the sign, what other products were there?

Breakers

Note two incentives planters had not to visit much flogging upon their slaves:

| Pic 349: Why is the slave woman wearing that bizarre looking collar?

Black belt

Responsorial preaching

Pic 350: Why do you think the planters entrusted mammies with their kids on such a wide scale?

'Peculiar institution'

Nat Turner's Rebellion

Amistad

Pic 351: Which direction are these slaves marching if they are marching to Tennessee?

| Why were Southern whites in a state of 'siege?'

American Colonization Society

Republic of Liberia

Monrovia

Quotes 351: Summarize William A. Smith's perspective on slavery:	| Summarize the perspective presented at the | American Anti-Slavery Society meeting: | | | | | |

Why didn't most African slaves want to go back to Africa when the Colonization Society began its transports?

Map 352: Note the states and territories by year they abolished slavery:	| Pic 352: What was | this tag used for? | | |

The Liberator

William Lloyd Garrison

American Anti-Slavery Society

Appeal to the Colored Citizens of the World

Sojourner Truth

Narrative of the Life of Frederick Douglass

Pg. 354: Examining the Evidence. What about American history does this map illuminate?

Pic 355: What about Sojourner Truth held audiences 'spellbound?'	| Pic 355 (r.): Where was Frederick Douglass posted at | the end of his career? | |

Mason-Dixon Line

Thinking Globally 356 – Categorize the countries by world region and the year they abolished slavery

Americas	*Europe*	*Middle East*	*Asia*

William Wilburforce

Summarize the pro-slavery argument regarding how comparatively bad Northern 'wage slaves' had it versus the more caring life of the Southern plantation:

| Pic 358: Do these pictures support or go against the idea that northern industrial work was worse than slavery?

Gag Resolution

Varying Viewpoints 359: What did the following historians have to say about slavery?

Ulrich Bonnell Phillips	*Frank Tannenbaum*	*Stanley Elkins*
Eugene Genovese	*Kenneth Stampp*	*Lawrence Levine*
Blassingame & Gutman	*Walter Johnson*	*Genovese, Jones & Morgan*
Philip D. Morgan	*Ira Berlin*	*David Brion Davis*

You must transcend the limitations of your mind and become one with the stream of history, for as a river flows, so flows the river of time. -Yoda

Quote 363: By what right- as in by what guiding force- does John O'Sullivan believe Americans are destined to rule the continent from sea to shining sea?

| What happened to President W.H. Harrison a month after taking office, who did *not* benefit from this tragedy, and why?

"Tyler Too"

One of the first things Clay and his Whig allies tried to get Tyler to do was to ascent to a new national bank- like the one Jackson killed. What happened?

"Fiscal Corporation"

"His Accidency"

Tariff of 1842

"Third War with England"

Caroline

Creole

Pic 365: Look closely at the words and the picture. How were the British characterizing the U.S.?

    In words: *In picture:*

Aroostook War

Map 366: If you were one of the delegates deciding on the Maine-Canada boundary, judging by the map what do you think the most natural lines would be?

Lone Star Republic

Summarize the foreign powers facing Texas in the run-up to 1840:

Summarize the perspectives on Texas held by the following:

James K. Polk   Henry Clay   John Tyler

_____

Pic 367: Compare this with the picture on pg. 312:

Similarities   Differences

_____

| Quote 367: What arguments did Brigadier Green have for supporting the Lone Star Republic? | When the authors write, "Americans were in a 'lick all creation' mood," what did they mean? |

Oregon Country

If you were a lawyer arguing the case, what would your main points be supporting the followings claims upon Oregon Country

Britain	Russia	USA	Indian tribes

Pic 368: Was the trip from this store out west difficult, according to the asterisked note at the bottom of the next page?

_____

Manifest Destiny

54-40 or Fight

The "Dark Horse"

Pic 370: This celebration of the white European settlers of North America and their unstoppable march over the entire continent can still be seen in:	If you were a lawyer arguing both sides, what would your main arguments be:
	Remove this painting *Keep it up where it is*

The "Mandate"

Walker Tariff

What were the things on President Polk's *Must List*?

1st

2nd

3rd

4th

Map 371: If you were deciding on the best place for a boundary for Oregon, what would you argue is most logical according to the map?

Pic 372: When was this fort handed over to the Americans?	What three population groups lived in California in 1845?

John Slidell

Slidell mission

Zachary Taylor

When Mexican soldiers (allegedly) crossed the Rio Grande, how did Polk respond?	When Americans sang, "Ho for the Halls of Montezuma," what did they mean?

Spot resolutions

Why were the Mexicans 'spoiling' to fight the Americans in turn?

___

Stephen W. Kearney ___

John C. Fremont ___

Bear Flag Republic ___

Winfield Scott ___

Map 374: The "disputed area," according to the map key, is what is now:

      a. Arizona   *b. New Mexico*   *c. Eastern Texas*   *d. Western Texas*

This June 14, 1845 event signaled the independence of California: _____

The first major battle of the Mexican-American War was at Monterrey in September of _____

While Kearny proceeded to Santa Fe and El Paso, winning the battles of _____

and _____ in December 1846, Mexico won its greatest victory of the war near

San Diego at _____. To reinforce the American claim over California and

support Fremont, Commodore John D. _____ left Mazatlan by sea for Monterey.

On land, Mexico's major resistance was defeated at the Battle of Buena Vista in February _____.

General Winfield Scott was dispatched from _____, landed at _____,

fought the Battle of Tampico in _____ and then bounced to _____

by sea before moving inland past Cerro Gordo to _____, where the war was

won in September of _____.

___

Nicholas Trist ___

Describe Trist's mission and what came of it:

___

Treaty of Guadalupe Hidalgo

"Conscience Whigs"

Contending Voices 375 - Summarize the views of the following:

    New York Evening Post   *Henry Clay*

With whom do you agree more?

How did the 'Anglo-Saxon spirit of fair play factor into the treaty?	Pic 376: This guy is most likely saying,
	a. unemployment just went down half a percent!
	b. dude, Scott just raised the Stars and Stripes over Mexico City!

The area ceded to the U.S. in the Treaty of Guadeloupe Hidalgo was Spanish territory for 282 years, Mexican territory for 26 years, and American territory for 168 years (as of 2016). To what extent do you think "long-memoried Mexicans" are right to view the U.S. as a "greedy bully?"

Wilmot Proviso

Why did Calhoun refer to Mexico as "forbidden fruit?"	Pic 377: Which soldier here would later be famous in the Civil War?

Pg. 379: What are some of the things the Californios did to become 'Makers of America?'

Quote 381: Webster warns here that: | What did politicians fear if the two political parties
                                            | became 'sectional'?

    a. 1776 will not be repeated |

                                            |

      b. easy come, easy go |

Popular sovereignty

Are you a true democrat in the Rousseauean sense (look up 'General Will of the People') and support the *idea* of popular sovereignty? Or do you think a greater force should prevail over the wishes of 'the people' when a moral issue you find offensive is at stake?

'Taylor fever'

Pic 382: When the U.S. invaded Iraq in 2003, many commentators around the world portrayed President Bush's popularity in the 2004 election in a way that was similar to this picture of Zachary Taylor. Many also portrayed President Obama this way when he was awarded the Nobel Peace Prize despite continuing war policies. In your opinion, should political leaders be subjected to this kind of scrutiny by the media, or should the media form less of an opposition and propagandize for the policies of the established politicians?

Free Soil Party

In what ways did the Free Soil Party reach out to disaffected members of the other parties?

Sutter's Mill

Gold Rush

Quote 383: Not only men went out west to Cali in '49, what kinds of sly women did as well?

Map 383: Gold Rush territory was in the   *a. south   b. center   c. north*   of California.

The Gold Mines had funny or offensive names at times. Categorize them into...

Named after places   *Named after people(s)*   *Named after verbs & adjectives*

Pic 384: In this picture, what is the process by which the gold is separated from the ore?

Underground Railroad

Pic 384: If it wasn't a literal railroad, why did they call it one? | Pic 385: Name the famous woman who was a leading 'stationmaster' on the Underground Railroad

---

Map 385: What was Texas' claim to the land shown here? | Was slavery ever allowed in Washington DC?

Summarize the 'twilight' moves of the three 'Senatorial Giants':

Henry Clay   *John C. Calhoun*   *Daniel Webster*   *Ralph Waldo Emerson (Quote 387)*

7th of March Speech

William Seward

Compromise of 1850

Chart 387: Note what the following got out of the Compromise:

The North   *The South*

Pic 388: What symbols can you find that suggest the artist approved of Clay's work as much as the Senators did?

Fugitive Slave Law

Map 389: The territories not opened to slavery included:

The territories that were open to slavery included:

How many representatives did the free states have? _____ Slave states? _____

Pic 390: How can you tell this cartoon was done by someone sympathetic to abolition?

Contending Voices 390 - Summarize the views of the following:

John C. Calhoun   *Daniel Webster*

With whom do you agree more?

Millard Fillmore

| Note the charges the Whigs laid on Franklin Pierce: | How did the Democrats respond? | Why did Scott lose in '52? |

Map 391: What year did your state abolish slavery? (If you live in the Old South, it's 1865): _____

| What was going on that led up to the Clayton-Bulwer Treaty? | Map 392: How many years would it be from 1850 to the year the U.S. acquired access to build the Panama Canal? |

Ostend Manifesto

Opium War

Treaty of Wanghia _____

"Most favored nation" status _____

"Extraterritoriality" _____

Matthew C. Perry _____

Treaty of Kanagawa _____

Pic 394: What evidence in the painting is there of the 'vivid impression' the gift from Perry made on this Japanese artist?

Gadsden Purchase _____

What was Jefferson Davis' rationale for sending Gadsden to make this offer to Mexico?	Had Mexico not agreed to sell the Gadsden land, this large city would likely not be American:

Stephen Douglas _____

Kansas-Nebraska Act _____

Map 396: The Union-Pacific Railroad runs through the current state of _____.

Pic 397: What was Douglas' rationale for forwarding the Kansas-Nebraska Act?

Republican Party _____

Quote 397: Sumner described the Kansas-Nebraska Act as:

What was his rationale for the following: _____

Why it was 'the worst'   _Why it was 'the best'_

"You know Toto, I don't think we're in Bleeding Kansas anymore."

Quote 399: In your opinion, are there any issues today in America that bring to mind this quote by Lincoln, that a "House divided against itself cannot stand?"

Uncle Tom's Cabin

Pic 400: What did Lincoln say to Harriet Beecher Stowe upon meeting her? | Pic 400 (r.): Why did Southerners say she didn't know what she was talking about?

Quote 400: What is the name of the brutal character in the novel? _____

Hinton Helper

Impending Crisis of the South

Pg. 401: Examining the Evidence. What sentimental value does the cabin represent in this passage?

New England Aid Company

Would you have been more swayed by the call of Whittier's song about making the west the homestead of the free, or the appeal to giving Southern rights to all that was a rejoinder?

Pic 403: By what actions did John Brown 'besmirch' the free soil cause?

Lecompton Constitution

James Buchanan

Bleeding Kansas

Map 402: List the battles in Kansas in order of when they happened:

Pic 404: Who is beating down who here, and where?

Who: Where: Why:

_____

Quote 404: How did the following view the beat down:

   Illinois State Journal   Petersburg Intelligencer

_____

Pic 405: Which groups in society supported the following and why:

                    Old Buck   The Pathfinder

Who:

Why:

_____

Map 406: Who finally won this election by | Who did your state vote for in 1856?
carrying the Southland and a few Northern states? |
                                                   |
                                                   |

_____

Dred Scott v. Stanford

Pic 407: Explain the Dred Scott case:

   Background: Legal issue at hand: Verdict:

_____

Quote 407: What did Chief Justice Roger Taney of the Supreme Court give as an explanation for the decision in the case?

_____

Panic of 1857

_____

Tariff of 1857

_____

Quote 408: During the 2016 election, businessman Donald Trump and | Pic 409: What was
socialist Bernie Sanders both advocated for high protective tariffs, as a | Lincoln's job in his
way to bring jobs back to the United States from cheaper overseas labor | 30s?
markets. Would Lincoln have agreed with their stance on this? |
                                                                       |

Lincoln-Douglas debates

Freeport Question

Freeport Doctrine

Pic 410: This was the first debate to be shown on TV:

a. true   b. false

| Quote 410: If a (white) presidential candidate said this today, what do you think the reaction would be?

Harpers Ferry

Contending Voices 411 - Summarize the views of the following:

Harriet Tubman   *Abraham Lincoln*

With whom do you agree more?

Pic 412: At the end when he was going to hang, John Brown   *a. was at peace   b. was irate*

Constitutional Union Party

Pic 413: The first president to play the new game of baseball was:

Chart 413: Did the election of the rail splitter ultimately split the Union?   *a. yes   b. no*

Map 414: In which Southern state did all the counties voted for the same candidate?

| What does it mean that Lincoln was a 'minority' president?

Quote 415: What was the Crittenden Compromise and why did it fail?

| Map 415: Which states voted by county unanimously for secession?

Confederate States of America

Jefferson Davis

Pic 416: The look of President Davis of the Confederacy seems: *a. serious*   *b. frivolous*

Quote 416: What was South Carolina's rationale for secession from the United States?

    Moral: *Legal:*

Quote 417: Did Lincoln follow Greeley's advice presented here?

Pic 417: Did Lincoln follow the American Eagle's advice presented here?

In his message to his congress, what did Jefferson Davis ask of the North?	By world standards, was the South all that different than other nationalist movements in the 1860s?
Quote 418 (right): How did the British view the Southern move to independence?	Do you agree with the parallels between the justification the colonists gave in '76 and what the Southerners gave in 1860?

Why did the parallels 'run even deeper'?

Varying Viewpoints 419: What did the following historians have to say about the Civil War?

    Nationalist School   *Charles & Mary Beard*   *J. Randall & A. Craven*

    A. Nevins & D. Potter   *E. Foner & E. Genovese*   *Ashworth & Lightner*

    Michael Holt   *With whom do you agree most?*

What's so civil about war anyway? –Guns n' Roses

Quote 421: Which minority group did Lincoln have in mind in this quote?

| What was symbolic in the way the Capitol dome looked when Lincoln was sworn in?

Was there a significant or logical natural border between the Federal territories and the Confederacy?

| Quote 421 (bot.): Why did Seward propose this half-joke scheme?

How did European powers such as Britain, France, Spain and others stand to *gain* from the U.S. Civil War?

| Pic 422: In which state (or former state) did the first shots of Civil War ring out?

Fort Sumter

Note the incidents that took place in the opening days of the war:

    April 12   *April 15*   *April 19*

Map 423: Note the following:

States that seceded before Fort Sumter	*States that seceded after*	*Slave states loyal to Union*
1	8	1
2	9	2
3	10	3
4	11	4
5		
6		
7		

Border States

West Virginia

How did Lincoln 'deal' with the Border States? | Quote 424: How did Lincoln feel about
                                                 | Kentucky?
                                                 |
                                                 |
                                                 |

Which side did the Indian tribes of Oklahoma favor and why? | Give an example of a family
                                                              | whose members fought on
                                                              | opposite sides of the war:
                                                              |
                                                              |
                                                              |_____

Contending Voices 424 - Summarize the views of the following:

   Horace Greeley   *Abe Lincoln*
                                       |
                                                                |
                                                                |
                                                                |
                                                                |
                                                                |

With whom do you agree more?

_____

Pic 425: Why are these two men 'friendly enemies?'

_____

Robert E. Lee _____

Thomas Stonewall Jackson _____

"Yeeeahhh!" _____

Chart 425: Divide the stats for the Southern states by the Total at bottom, and list the percentage of what the South had vis-à-vis the North:

Manufacturing establishments   *Capital invested*   *Laborers*   *Value of Products*

_____

Pg. 426: What are some of the things 'Billy Yank' and 'Johnny Reb' did to become 'Makers of America'?

_____

_____

Pic 428: What were some of the new technologies deployed in the Civil War?

___

Ulysses S. Grant

Quote 429: Which side did most British commoners sympathize with according to the American minister? | Why didn't the South get the foreign help it counted on during the Civil War?

Pic 429: Which four ethnic immigrants did this poster target? | From what other sources did Britain gain the cotton fibers it needed for its textile industry?

Pic 430: What does this cartoon have to do with "Old King Cotton's dead and buried; brave young Corn is King?

___

Trent Affair

Alabama

Laird rams

Dominion of Canada

Jefferson Davis

Writ of habeas corpus

Pic 432: What is distinctive about the way Abe Lincoln dressed? | Pic 433: The chances that an amputee lived were about _____ percent.

The Draft

How did some rich boys get out of serving? | Pic 433 (bot.): Why did the Irish lynch blacks in New York?

New York draft riots

Chart 434: Was there ever a time when the South had as many fighters as the North? _____

Morrill Tariff Act

Greenbacks

National Banking System

How many years had it been since Jackson killed the 'monster bank' to when Congress authorized the National Banking System?	How many years would it be before this would be replaced by the Federal Reserve system in 1913?

Runaway inflation

Pic 435: Would you feel comfortable if you went to a friend's house and they had these potholders in the kitchen- or would you be cool with that if they told you they were made as a fundraiser?

Homestead Act

'Government girls'

U.S. Santiary Commission

Clara Barton

Did you miss anyone? Go back and find out the role of these people in this heady era:

Dorothea Dix

Elizabeth Blackwell

Sally Tompkins

Charles Francis Adams

Napoleon III

Maximilian

Now these are such sad times / that we're all living in / for killing your brother / is the mightiest sin.   -Waylon Jennings

Quote 438: Lincoln's paramount objective in fighting the Civil War was to end slavery: *T*   *F*

Manassas Junction

Note the kind of parade heading out to Bull Run: | Summarize what happened at Bull Run:

Pic 439 & Quote 438: What kind of condition were the Federal soldiers in 1) as they were leaving Washington, and 2) after the Battle of Bull Run:

Before   *After*

George McClellan

Army of the Potomac

Note some of McClellan's virtues: *Note some of his defects:*

Peninsula Campaign

Jeb Stuart

Map 440: Before moving toward Richmond, McClellan took this Virginia city _____

This major battle was won by the Confederates on early July, 1862 _____

Quote 441: Lincoln's reply to McClellan's request | This Confederate soldier characterized
after the Battle of the Seven Days can be described as: | the scene on the battlefield as:

   a. good humored   *b. agitated* | *a. glorious*   *b. disgusting*

What did the term 'total war' mean to Union strategy? | Map 441: During 1862, this Union
                                                       | general marched south to Vicksburg:

Monitor

Merrimack

Pic 442: What was so special about this particular battle that it changed the nature of naval warfare?

Blockade

Second Bull Run

John Pope

Antietam

Emancipation Proclamation

Pic 444: Describe the important consequences of Antietam:

Did Abraham Lincoln really free any slaves? If you were a lawyer arguing each side, what would your main points be?

Lincoln freed all the slaves	*Lincoln freed some slaves*	*Lincoln freed no slaves at all*

Thirteenth Amendment

Contending Voices 445 - Summarize the views of the following:

Cincinnati Enquirer	*Lincoln*

Map 445: How did Lincoln's policy change regarding the state buying the slaves from their owners?

Why did the 'Democratic rhymester' think Lincoln didn't deserve the name 'Honest Abe'?

'Abolition war'

Pic 446: The Massachusetts 54th, the subject of the movie *Glory*, saw action at this battle:

Robert G. Shaw

No black soldiers ever fought for the Confederacy   *True*   *False*

Quote 446: Lincoln thought highly of black soldiers' fighting ability   *True*   *False*

Ambrose Burnside

Fredericksburg

Chancellorsville

Joseph Hooker

George C. Meade

George Pickett

Pickett's Charge

Gettysburg Address

Map 448: Gettysburg is   *N   S   W   E*   of Washington D.C.

During Pickett's Charge, Confederate forces clashed against these Union positions:

Pg. 450: Examining the Evidence. What about American history does this item illuminate?

Pic 449: Which of these guys is on the $50 bill? _____

Map 451: Grant's strategy in Tennessee is viewed as   *a. successful*   *b. a failure*

Forts Henry and Donelson _____

Shiloh _____

David G. Farragut _____

Vicksburg _____

Quote 451: What other part of the country had thoughts of secession and independence?

_____

Chattanooga _____

William T. Sherman _____

What were the following slang for:

    Sherman's Blue Bellies   *Sherman's Sentinels*   *Sherman's Hairpins*

_____

Sherman's March to the Sea _____

Map 452: After Atlanta, when Sherman actually made it to the sea, where was he? _____

Quote 453: Before you make fun of this letter's grammar and spelling, do you think this Rebel soldier, probably 18-years-old and not graduated from school, would have been happy to know that as he lay dying on the battlefield, his last letter would appear in the most used history textbook in the country 150 years later? Argue whether you think he would have been happy to know that or not:

_____

C.C. on the C. of the W. _____

Copperheads _____

Clement Vallandigham _____

The Man Without a Country _____

Union Party _____

Salmon Chase _____

Pic 454: Sherman's march can be described as   *a. effective*   *b. brutal*   *c. both*

Pic 455 (top): Summarize what women were doing during the war according to this blurb:	Pic 455 (bot.): In this cartoon, McClellan is portrayed as
	a. one-sided *b. a voice of reason*

Wilderness Campaign

Battle of Cold Harbor

Map 456: So... how'd the Democrats do in this election? _____

Map 457: Lee surrendered at Richmond after Grant took the city: *T*   *F*

Appomattox Courthouse

This was one term of surrender considered generous:	Lee admonished his soldiers not to cheer in the faces of the Confederates for this reason:

Pic 458: What happened to the Confederate capital at the end of the war?

Ford's Theater

John Wilkes Booth

Andrew Johnson

Pic 459: How can you tell this is an event of national mourning?

Thinking Globally 460: What is nationalism according to this article?

Varying Viewpoints 463: What did the following have to say about the consequences of this war?

Eric Foner   *James McPherson*   *D.G. Faust*   *Thomas Cochran*

If we don't fight about race, then it's about gender, or class, or religion, or sports or brand names, or... wait, is there anything we don't fight about?

Quote 465: Lincoln's message at his second inaugural address was spoken in a tone of:

　　a. vengeance　　　　b. reconciliation　　　　c. hostility

Were the Confederate leaders rounded up and put on trial? What happened to them?	What do the authors mean when they write: "Not only an age had perished, but a civilization had collapsed... gone with the wind"?

Describe the condition of the Old South after the war:

"Your Government"

Exodusters

Pic 466: Describe how Charleston looked at the end of the war:	Pic 467: About how many children are attending this schoolhouse?

Pg. 468: Examining the Evidence. What about American history does this item illuminate?

Freedman's Bureau

Pic 470: Why did Andrew Johnson face impeachment as is illustrated here?

"10 Percent" Plan

Wade-Davis Bill

Pocket veto

Chart 471: How did legal notions about Reconstruction evolve over the following years:

1864-1865   *1865-1866*   *1866-1867*   *1867-1877*

| Why were some of the Radicals secretly please when Lincoln was assassinated? | Summarize Johnson's stance on how to treat the defeated South: |

Black Codes

| Quote 472: According to this Georgian, whites and blacks had | Pic 472: Was sharecropping more like slavery or more like getting a job at a farm? Explain your opinion. |

a. good   b. bad

relations following the conclusion of the conclusion of the Civil War.

Pacific Railroad Act

Civil Rights Bill

Contending Voices 473 - Summarize the views of the following:

Thaddeus Stevens   *James Lawrence Orr*

With whom do you agree more?

Fourteenth Amendment

Reconstruction Act

Pic 475: What did T. Stevens mean when he said Southern institutions must be 'revolutionized?'

Military Reconstruction

Map 476: Note the former Confederate states in each military district:

District 1	District 2	District 3	District 4	District 5

Fifteenth Amendment

Ex Parte Milligan

"Bluebellies"

"Redeemers"

Woman's Loyal League

Quote 478: Why were women seeking social equality and voting rights, like Susan B. Anthony, disappointed with Reconstruction era suffrage reform?

Union League

Scalawags

Carpetbaggers

Pic 478: Why did the event shown constitute a political and social 'revolution' in the South?

Pic 479: Was Congressman John Lynch successful in integrating public accommodations?

Ku Klux Klan

Pic 480: The goals of the Ku Klux Klan were: Southern whites supported them because:

Force Acts

Tenure of Office Act

Pic 481: What was this ticket for and why was it in such high demand?

_____

Seward's Folly

Map 482: Alaska is   *bigger*   *the same size*   *smaller*   than Texas.

While today we know Alaska was a great deal because of all the resources it has there, why did Congress authorize Seward's purchase back then?

_____

Quote 482: What was the state of the freed slave according to Fredrick Douglass?

_____

Pic 483: Thomas Nast (better known as the guy who first drew Santa Claus in his modern clothes and with his portly physique) also drew this, which said that ex-slaves during Reconstruction:

a. were fine and it was a great day for freedom   *b. things were not all that great despite freedom*

Was Reconstruction successful or a failure? If you were a lawyer arguing both sides, what arguments would you trot out in support of your position?

> *Reconstruction was a success*   *Reconstruction was a failure*

Varying Viewpoints 483: What did the following historians have to say about Reconstruction?

William Dunning   *Howard Beale*   *W.E.B. Dubois*

Kenneth Stampp   *Benedict & Litwack*   *Eric Foner*   *Steven Hahn*

Pg. 488   **23 – POLITICAL PARALYSIS IN THE GILDED AGE**   **Machine hack** _____

Disagreement? In American history? Nah, can't be true.

Quote 488: Did Henry Adams believe in the Theory of Progress?	Do you? Should each president be better than the last?

Adams was bringing up perhaps the most nerve-wracking idea of the times, *Degeneration Theory.* The theory said it isn't progress that happens in civilized societies, it's anti-progress. As time moves forward within a civilization that exists in an advanced state, as ours has since the Industrial Age, the regular processes that affect people in their natural state apply less and less. Natural selection no longer applies, so the weak survive as well as the strong, reproduce, and with votes, impose upon the strong and vital. We are now living artificially, the theory says, in the society of comfort and ease which we have constructed around ourselves. And within that bubble, indeed there was no 'Washington' around during the Reconstruction era, 'Grants' were. There was no Washington to take the lead, because there literally was *no* Washington, his own descendants being less than he. And in our day? Degeneration theory predicts we weaken morally, mentally and physically as time has gone by, instead of strengthen. If you don't believe it, Google: "Thomas Jefferson's letters" and read one. Or imagine why we *could* and *did* go to the Moon 50 years ago but not today. So what did *waving the bloody shirt* mean? And what did it have to do with 'mob mentality?'

Remember the "Era of Good Feelings?" What did the "Era of Good Stealings" mean for the country?

Tweed ring

Pic 489: Boss Tweed was in charge of this public institution, but unofficially: _____

Credit Mobilier scandal

"Turn the Rascals Out"

Panic of 1873

Pic 490: This image, reminiscent of an *ouroborus*, an old symbol of a dragon that eats its own tail, shows who? And why are they consuming each other?	Quote 492: What does Wells think about the economic crisis of '73?

Gilded Age

Patronage

James G. Blaine

Pic 493: Why would one guess that Union soldier-veterans would vote Republican in '76?

Rutherford B. Hayes

Compromise of 1877

Map 494: Which candidate did the South vote for in the majority? _____

Chart 494: Which body actually cast the deciding vote in the election of 1876? _____

Civil Rights Act

Sharecropping

Jim Crow Laws

Plessy v. Ferguson

Pic 495: How did Hayes encourage the possibility of segregation and Jim Crow in the South, whether he agreed with the policies or not?

Map 496: Draw both the before and after charts of a common Southern plantation:

Pic 496: What message do you think this kind of public execution was meant to send?

Chart 497: More whites than blacks were lynched (hung) before the year _____

The number of both races being 0 lynched did not occur until the year _____

Pic 497: What kinds of problems began occurring between whites and Chinese in California at this time that led to incidents like this one on the magazine cover?

Chinese Exclusion Act

U.S. vs. Wong Kim Ark

Pendleton Act

Contending Voices 499 - Summarize the views of the following:

Washington Plunkitt   Theodore Roosevelt

With whom do you agree more?

Pg. 500: What are some of the things Chinese did to become 'Makers of America'?

Mudslinging

How did mudslinging help Grover Cleveland in this election?

| Pic 503: What logic was used to argue for the protective tariff and would you have been swayed to be for or against it?

Pic 504: Aside from this novelty, note some of the humorous slogans used for things going on during this election of 1888:

Billion-Dollar Congress

Pic 504: Today we say the government appoints a 'czar' this or a 'czar' that, a 'drug czar' or a 'food czar' or 'health czar', but where did the use of this term come from?

_____

Thomas Reed _____

Chester Arthur _____

James A. Garfield _____

Pic 505: Why were the strikers mad during the Homestead Strike?

_____

Map 506: Who won the 1892 election?   Was this the person the South voted for?

_____   _____

Populists _____

Grandfather clause _____

Pic 507 (top): This group of populists was   In your opinion, who was right in all this?
brought to heel by which organization?

Thomas A. Watson _____

Pic 507: After failing to get the two races to cooperate, | What happened to gold deposits in the
what was Watson's stance at the end of his life? | government treasury around 1893?

Varying Viewpoints 509: What did the following historians have to say about populism?

Twain & Warner   _Charles A. Beard_   _John D. Hicks_   _R. Hofstadter_   _C. Vann Woodward_

Lawrence Goodwyn   _Edward Ayers_   _Robert C. McMath_   _Charles Postel_   _Eric Rauchway_

Quote 512: Henry George would most likely favor:

a. laissez-faire economics   b. a degree of government socialism   c. libertarianism

What does the tongue-in-cheek phrase, "The iron colt becomes the iron horse" mean in this case?

_____

Cleveland came under criticism for his "giveaway" of 1887, what did he "give away" and is the term a fair assessment?

_____

Chart 513: After the U.S., which country in the Americas had the most railways in 1889? _____ Where would India be classified on this table?	List the top 6 countries in Europe by amount of railway in 1889: 1) 2) 3) 4) 5) 6)

Map 514: No one likes the concept of eminent domain, whereby the government can seize the private property of a citizen by force for a supposed national good (though in fairness they pay you the market price or more), but looking at the map, could the railroad (or later the highway system) have been constructed without eminent domain being invoked? Why or why not?

_____

In the poem on pg. 515, what is a 'Paddy'?	What are the 'Paddies' doing?

Pic 515: Where do you think the toughest place to build railroads would be? _____

_____

Pic 516: In what year did the 'Great Event' occur on the Union Pacific RR? _____

Quote 516: James B. Weaver was   *a. a supporter of the rail companies   b. a populist*

Pic 517: Describe the ceremony in Utah during the connection of the Transcontinental Railroad:

_____

How was 'time itself' bent to the needs of the railway system?

Time zones

Jay Gould

Pic 518: What is the meaning of 'robber baron' in this context? | Are there any 'robber barons'
| today? Do you have an example?
|
|

What happened in the *Wabash, St. Louis & Pacific Railroad Company v. Illinois* case?

Interstate Commerce Act

Quote 519: What is Ralph Waldo Emerson (Seriously? This guy's *still* around?) saying happens to German and Irish Americans who go to work on the railroad?

You know what a millionaire is, but when was it first employed as a term to describe people?

Chicago became a major 'break-of-bulk' node (a place where forms of transportation switch for those of you who didn't take AP Human Geography and if you didn't then shame on you!). What about Chicago's location made it a break-of-bulk city- and what forms of transport were products switching between?

Captain of Industry

Note some of the new inventions that appeared at this time, often in conjunction with industrialization:

Pic 520: Who was the 'Wizard of Menlo Park' and what kinds of things did he invent?

Andrew Carnegie

John D. Rockefeller

J.P. Morgan

Vertical integration

Horizontal integration

Trust

Standard Oil

Interlocking directorates

Pic 521: Does this image about the influence over government and other businesses by Standard Oil also apply to J.P. Morgan's banking empire? Why or why not?

Heavy industry

Capital goods

Consumer goods

Bessemer process

Why is Andrew Carnegie's life considered a 'rags-to-riches' story?	Quote 522: Do you agree with Carnegie on this? (Or are you going to be buried in a solid gold coffin?)

Pic 522: While Carnegie and Rockefeller were producing physical goods, what was Morgan producing that is considered 'finance capitalism?'	Pic 523: The cartoonist believes people like Rockefeller *a. respect politicians* *b. uh, no*

What circumstances brought Carnegie and Morgan 'into collusion', and what resulted?

The invention that gave the oil industry a 'new lease on life' at the turn of the 20th century was:

Gospel of wealth

Social darwinists

Which social darwinist was American?   *a. Herbert Spencer*   *b. William Graham Sumner*

Why did social darwinists take to the laissez-faire economics theory of David Ricardo so readily?

'Survival of the fittest'

Pic 524: The image of the big capitalist fat cat lazily sitting atop the mass of working people who support them, like this cartoonist is describing as a social commentary about Vanderbilt and the others, is a classic image.

What is his opinion of their amazing wealth?   Do you agree? Or do the wealthy people of the the world work hard to get that way as well?

Plutocracy

Sherman Anti-Trust Act

Contending Voices 525 - Summarize the views of the following:

> *Populist platform*   *Social darwinists*

With whom do you agree more?

Pic 526: How are these images an example of 'gross inequality'? | Do you think the family on the left should be | obligated to give money to families like the one | on the right?

Quote 526: Grady was sad because the Confederate veteran: *a. died in an accident   b. died poor*

'Hillbillies'

Pic 527: Who is doing a lot of the mill work?	Chart 527: As the South made more 'spindles' England also grew in its industry: *a. true* *b. false*

Chart 528: By 1903, the U.S.   *a. dominated*   *b. fell behind*   in the world cotton industry.

Pic 528: Are these women the 'new women' of Charles Dana Gibson's artistic ideal?	The Polish workers who got this work schedule to follow might have understood your schedule. Rewrite the ditty replacing their terms for your terms, like 'alarm' instead of 'whistle':
Map 529: Name three states where 25% of the Was working in manufacturing: _____ _____ _____	
What industries and natural resources were located in Ohio? _____	
Which industries and natural resources were located in your state? (if you live in Ohio, move and then finish this assignment). (we're waiting)	Do you think all these bells and whistles got us used to school bells and informed our ideas about how schools should be run?

Pic 530 (top): Do you like the idea of the 'Gibson Girl', who is assertive and interested in activities like sports and being in fashion?	Pic 530 (bot.): Whose life would you rather have- Gibson Girl or Breaker Boy?

Philanthropy

'Scabs'

"Lockout"

What did Jay Gould boast he could do to keep workers in line?

Labor union

Pg. 531: Examining the Evidence. What about American history does this item illuminate?

"Black list"

Company town

Pic 532: What evidence is there in this Koehler painting that a strike is happening?

National Labor Union

Knights of Labor

Why does the little song on pg. 533 have the term 'eight hours' in it?

Haymarket Square

AFL

Mother Jones

Samuel Gompers

Pic 536: Do you agree or disagree with Gompers that workers should have the right to strike if the firm they work for doesn't give in to their demands in a collective bargaining scenario?

| Could the students at *your* school strike? They would have to agree not to do the work until their demands were met, like better cafeteria food or whatever. It would make the news. What other issue could they strike about?

Varying Viewpoints 537: What did the following historians have to say about industrialization?

Matthew Josephson   *Gutman & Montgomery*   *Alexis de Tocqueville*

Stephan Thernstrom   *James Henretta*   *Michael Katz*

Sip an espresso at a café in an Art Deco district and talk about a Monet painting while Debussy is playing in the background. You'll have "arrived."

Quote 539: If Lyman Abbott is right and the condition of our cities affects the whole country and our psyches, how do you think he would evaluate the Americans of today based on their cities?

_____

How many people did New York have in 1900? | What was its ranking worldwide?

_____

Skyscraper _____

"Form follows function" _____

Note some new developments in transportation at the turn of the 20th century:

_____

Map 540: In 1900, the biggest three cities in America were:

_____   _____   _____

In 1900, the biggest three cities in Europe were:

_____   _____   _____

In 1900, the biggest three cities in the rest of the world were:

_____   _____   _____

Chart 540: After which year did the percentage of Americans living in cities pass 80%? _____

Pic 541: Note some of the interesting things about the Brooklyn Bridge:

_____

Department store _____

What happened to the volume of waste generated by city-dwellers in this era?

_____

Dumbbell tenement _____

Which ethnic groups were classified as 'New Immigrants?' | Pic 542: How many rooms had
| access to sunlight in a tenement?

If you were a lawyer arguing immigration policy, and in your appearance before Congress you brought the Graph 543 to address a subcommittee deciding on a new bill, which two decades of the graph would you argue should be mimicked during the next two decades and why?

_____

Chart 543: Which nations did the Old Immigration come from versus the New Immigration?

Old: *New:*

_____

Pg. 545: What are some of the things Italians did to become 'Makers of America'?

_____

_____

_____

Pic 546: America's cities like New York were: Quote 546: This lady is _____ to come to the U.S.

                                                    |
a. densely   *b. sparsely*   populated in 1900. | *a. ambivalent*   *b. sad*   *c. ecstatic*

Pic 547: While they assimilated, note some ways that Jewish, Polish and Italian immigrants held on to their traditional cultures in this era:

Pg. 548: Examining the Evidence. What about American history does this item illuminate?

_____

_____

_____

Jane Addams _____

Hull House _____

Pic 549: What age groups gathered at Hull House for cultural events?

_____

Settlement houses _____

Florence Kelley _____

Nativism

Do you agree with the nativists that America, if it accepts too many immigrants, becomes a dumping ground instead of a melting pot?

| Pic 550: Did immigrants automatically favor high immigration levels?

What were some specific complaints the Nativists had about the new immigrants?

| Quote 551: What was Israel Zangwill's take on the high levels of new immigration?

Pic 551: What did the people of France get the people of America for its 100th birthday celebration?

Contending Voices 551 - Summarize the views of the following:

Henry Cabot Lodge   Grover Cleveland

What political factors may be playing into these opinions?   With whom do you agree more?

Emma Lazarus

What did the nativists think about Emma Lazarus' poem inscribed on the Statue of Liberty?

Liberal protestants

What two new Christian denominations appeared at this time?

YMCA

Pic 552: What city is this large service for workers taking place in? _____

Charles Darwin

Darwin promoted natural selection, summarize how it was different than belief in divine creation of fixed species:

Normal schools

| Describe the rise in the literacy rate between 1870 and 1900 in America: | Pic 554: What did Booker T. Washington advocate? |

Tuskegee Institute

George Washington Carver

W.E.B. DuBois

NAACP

"Talented tenth"

| Pic 555: Have you ever considered renouncing your citizenship? What country would you move to? | Quote 555: What 'double consciousness' is DuBois describing here? |

Land-grant colleges

Chart 556: As a percentage of high school graduates, more Americans graduated from college in:

    a. 1880   *b. 1920*   *c. 2000*   *d. 2011*

Name three universities that philanthropists, despite their sometimes unsavory reputations, donated money to open:

| How was Johns Hopkins University different than the others?

Note three examples highlighting how colleges and universities secularized in this era:

1)   2)   3)

William James _____

Pragmatism _____

Library of Congress _____

They say Andrew Carnegie came from Scotland at age 13 with $2 in his pocket. Note his amazing contribution to the poor man's education:

Pic 558: What is a good example of the "penny press?"
_____

William Randolph Hearst _____

Yellow journalism _____

Joseph Pulitzer _____

Edwin Godkin _____

Henry George _____

Edward Bellamy _____

Pic 559: Would Victoria Woodhall and Tennessee Chaflin have agreed with Antony Comstock on the Comstock Law? Why or why not?

Pg. 560: What are some of the things the Pragmatists did to become 'Makers of America'?

_____

_____

_____

What affect on birthrates did moving to the growing America have? Why?

_____

Chart 562: In general, what has been the trend in Americans getting divorced?	In which decade did 50 percent of marriages begin ending in divorce?

Jane Addams
_____

NAWSA
_____

Carrie Chapman Catt
_____

Map 564: In which part of the country did women have the most voting rights before the Nineteenth Amendment granted all American women suffrage?

_____

National Prohibition Party
_____

WCTU
_____

ASPCA
_____

Who began the Red Cross and what is this organization?

_____

Lew Wallace
_____

Horatio Alger
_____

Realism
_____

Mark Twain
_____

Henry James
_____

Quote 566: What did Hemingway think of Twain's writing?	Pic 566: Twain's: real name was	Quote 567: James argued realist writing should:

Naturalism
_____

Stephen Crane _____

Jack London _____

Regionalism _____

Bret Harte _____

How did the following influence the realist and regionalist movements in art and sound?

Thomas Eakins   _Winslow Homer_   _James Whistler_

John Singer Sargent   _Augustus Saint-Gaudens_   _Thomas Edison_

Pic 568: What is the deeper meaning behind this piece?	Pic 569: Why was Chicago called the "White City" at the turn of the century?

City Beautiful movement _____

Note the contributions of the following to urban planning and (re)development:

Baron Haussmann   _Daniel Burnham_   _Frederick Law Olmsted_

World's Columbia Expedition _____

Pic 570: What new transportation device appeared at this time?	Do you have one of these?

Wild West shows _____

Buffalo Bill Cody _____

Annie Oakley _____

P.T. Barnum & J.A. Bailey _____

Where and when did baseball start?   Where and when did boxing start?

What makes a nation's pillars high, and its foundations strong? What makes it mighty to defy, the foes that round it throng?
Not gold but only men can make, a people great and strong; Men who for truth and honor's sake, stand fast and suffer long.
Brave men who work while others sleep, who dare while others fly, they build a nation's pillars deep, and lift them to the sky. -Emerson

Quote 574: Both Frederick Jackson Turner and Washakie agree that the story of America is:

    a. a equal distribution of land between races   *b. the conquest of an entire continent*

Note some of the wars between Indian groups happening on the Great Plains and in the Southwest:

| Pic 575: which large mammal
| probably wishes the Indians
| never acquired the horse from
| the Spanish:

What effect did whites pioneering out west into the new territories have on the Indians there?

Reservation system

What gory events happened in the following run-ups to the Battle of the Little Bighorn:

    Sand Creek Massacre   *Fetterman Massacre*

Battle of the Little Bighorn

Great Sioux Reservation

George Armstrong Custer

Pic 576: Why did the | Map 577: Note the modern day states and the years for these Indian battles:
Pawnee support the |
U.S. settlers and |

	Year	Event	State		Year	Event	State
military forces?							
	_____	Camp Grant	_____		_____	Salt River	_____
	_____	Red River	_____		_____	Little Bighorn	_____
	_____	Bear Paw	_____		_____	Wounded Knee	_____

Pic 578 & 579: Note the roles of the following Indian warriors:

    Crazy Horse   *Sitting Bull*   *Geronimo*   *Red Cloud*

Buffalo Bill Cody

Ghost Dance

Battle of Wounded Knee

Contending Voices 580 – How did each think about the dance and the massacre that followed:

    James McLaughlin   *Chief Black Elk*

Who do you agree with more?

Dawes Severality Act

Quote 580: Why was Plenty Coups sad?	Map 581: About what percent of the American landmass is set aside for Indian reservations?

"Fifty-Niners"

Comstock Lode

Pg. 582: What are some of the things the Plains Indians did to become 'Makers of America'?

Mining industry

"Beef bonanza"

The Long Drive

Wild Bill Hickok

Map 585: Turn this paper sideways and label the origin and destination points for the cattle trails:

Gulf of
Mexico

```
                                                         /-------\
        /eastern boundary of open range--------------------------/      \        /
------------------/                                                   ------------------/
```

Rocky Mts.

What were some hazards on the Long Drive?

Cowboy

Graph 586: About what year set the record for amount of acres homesteaded?	What kind of fraud was perpetrated doing this?

Map 587: Note the annual rainfall and the type of agricultural products in the following:

State	Rainfall	Products	State	Rainfall	Products
Western Washington			Iowa		
Northeastern Nevada			Wisconsin		
New Mexico			Your State		

Map 588: Note the percentage of the following states that are federal land:

State	Percentage federal land	State	Percentage federal land
Rhode Island		New York	
Virginia		Your State	
State with smallest %		State with biggest %	

Sooners

Eighty-niners

"The Frontier"

Pg. 590: Examining the Evidence. What about American history does this item illuminate?

After subduing the Indians, Anglo-Americans clashed in the Southwest with this group that has become its biggest historic rival for dominance of the New World:	In 1892, this store sent out a catalog, ushering in a new age of shopping:

Mechanization of agriculture

Thinking Globally 592 –
What is the Turner thesis?

Summarize how the following have a similar ethos of pioneering
what does their version of 'Manifest Destiny' look like?

Canadians:

Argentines:

Russians:

Afrikaner Boers:

Pic 594: Despite inflation, the Medieval farmer Would probably be _____ seeing this picture: a. jealous b. haughty	Quote 594: The author of this is expressing a. happiness b. melancholy sadness

Tenant farmers

The Grange

Pic 596: What were the 'fundamental premises' of these populist farmers?

Farmers' Alliances

Populists

Pic 597: What similarity did the rhetoric of Mary Elizabeth Lease have with that of Patrick Henry?

Jacob Coxey

Pic 598: Coxey's Army marched to _____ | What was Eugene V. Debs role
under slogans like: | in the Pullman Strike
|
|
|

Pullman Strike

Pic 599: Did President Cleveland support Debs or Olney? What happened to end the strike?

'Golden McKinley'

'Silver Bryan'

Marcus Alonzo Hanna

Pic 600: What happened to the opposition that opened the way for McKinley to win?

Pic 601: Would plowholders or bondholders be more likely to agree with the message of this cartoon? Why? What was the difference between the two?

Fourth party system

Pic 603 (bot.): What did each of these campaign propaganda 'gimcracks' promise?

Gold Standard Act

Varying Viewpoints 604: How did the following argue on the subject of the Frontier?

Turner   Limerick, White & Worster

Imagine if there was a Ferris wheel so big you could see back in time & look over the flow of ages past as it becomes our own age. Cool.

Quote 607: The Democratic platform in 1900 favored:

      a. Washington's advice on avoiding foreign entanglements   *b. interventionism*

How did American foreign policy shift suddenly at this juncture in history?

_____

What was Josiah Strong's book called and what did it advocate?	Quote 607: Does this WaPo editorial agree or disagree with Strong? Cite evidence:

Uncle Sam

Pic 608: Noticing the 'menu' on this imperial menu, which places is Uncle Sam deciding on?

Alfred Thayer Mahan

Big Sister Policy

American Samoa

Quote 609: Secretary of State Olney's message to Britain can best be described as:	Pic 609: Note some reasons given in this cartoon for the U.S. and Britain to stay peaceful:
a. humble *b. bombastic*	

Great Rapprochement

McKinley Tariff

Liliuokalani

Pic 610: What was Queen Liliuokalani's opinion of Hawaii as an American territory?	Quote 611: Decide on an adjective to describe the tone of this Spanish newspaper:

Insurrectos

Henry Cabot Lodge

Battleship Maine

Map 611: Place a _Yes_ in the line of the U.S. annexed or otherwise gained the territory and a _no_ if it was just a place where an overseas issue occurred involving the U.S. in this time:

_____ _Beijing_   _____ _Philippines_   _____ _Guam_   _____ _Samoa_

_____ _Hawaii_   _____ _Alaska_   _____ _Chile_   _____ _Venezuela_

_____ _Cuba_   _____ _Puerto Rico_   _____ _Wake Is._   _____ _Midway Is._

Pic 612: What was the role of the 'Yellow Press' in getting the U.S. to enter into the Spanish-American War?

_____

_____

Teller Amendment

Theodore Roosevelt

George Dewey

Map 613: What two events happened in Manila Bay, in chronological order?

1) _____ 2) _____

Emilio Aguinaldo

Because he was worried about Japan annexing Hawaii, what did President McKinley do?

_____

William R. Shafter

Rough Riders

Pic 614: Why did the Americans later regret they allied with Aguinaldo in the Philippines?

| Map 615: Leaving Tampa, Florida on a hot June
| day (Roosevelt and the Rough Riders stayed
| at what is now the onion-domed University of
| Tampa building), what was their destination?
|
|

Map 615 (inset): the three major land battles were:

What kinds of tropical problems made it so the Americans counted their blessings that this was a short war?

| Note the number of casualties in the war:

What happened to Puerto Rico after the conclusion of the Spanish-American War?

| Why did the Americans have a dilemma with the Philippines?

Pic 616: Because of the Spanish-American War and the Philippine-American War, the U.S. suddenly:

        a. set all the peoples free   *b. was unsure of what to do with the former Spanish lands*

Quote 616: What did President McKinley conclude about the best course of action for the Philippines?

Anti-Imperialist League

What did Kipling mean by the 'White Man's Burden' in the poem?

| Did the Anti-Imperialist League agree that the U.S. should 'take up the burden'

Contending Voices 617 - Summarize the views of the following:

    Albert Beveridge   *George F. Hoar*

With whom do you agree more?

Pg. 618: What are some of the things the Puerto Ricans did to become 'Makers of America'?

Foraker Act

Insular Cases

Platt Amendment

Guantanamo

Pic 620: What visual evidence is there in this image of the idea that this was a 'Splendid Little War' like John Hay said? | Pic 621: What happened in the Philippines at this point?

Philippine-American War

William Howard Taft

By the turn of the century: *a. Japan was rising and China was declining   b. the opposite*

Open Door note

Boxer Rebellion

Pic 623: What does 'Columbia's' liking of her new 'Easter Bonnet' say about American public opinion in 1900?

Pg. 624: What are some of the things the Filipinos did to become 'Makers of America'?

The two Ps

Pic 626: Which organization carried out the unique feat of blasting out this part of the Panama Canal? | Pic 626 (bot.): The youngest president so far in American history has been:
|
| *a. Kennedy   b. Obama   c. Roosevelt*

Hay-Paunceforte Treaty

Pic 628: How did TR manage to 'Speak Softly and Carry a Big Stick' to get Colombia and Panama to agree to the U.S. building of the Canal?

Roosevelt Corollary

What was the reason for Russia's aggressive move to take Port Arthur in Manchuria, China?	What was Japan's response?	Finally, what was TR's role in arbitration?

Thinking Globally 630 – How did the following ideas serve to rationalize and justify imperialism?

The Maxim Gun   Self-Sustaining Empires   Mission Civilisatrice   Kultur

Map 631: List the imperial holdings of the following Great Powers:

Germany   France   Great Britain   Russia

Netherlands

Italy   Belgium

Spain   Japan   United States   Portugal

Yellow Peril

Root-Takahira agreement

Varying Viewpoints 633: How did the following characterize American imperialism?

Julius Pratt   Howard Beale   Paul Kramer   Williams & LaFeber   Recent

No more fooling around- its time to make things materially better

Quote 638: To TR, what does the term 'square deal' actually mean?

_____

Progressivism

What kind of social commentary did the following authors give in their books?

H.D Lloyd	Thorstein Veblen	Jacob A. Riis	T. Dreiser

_____

Pic 639: How does this picture illustrate the concept of America as a 'melting pot?'

_____

Social gospel

Muckrakers

Contending Voices 640 - Summarize the views of the following:

       TR   *Ida Tarbell*

Were the muckrakers a help or hindrance to reform?   *With whom do you agree more?*

_____

Pic 640: What three adjectives come to mind first when you see this picture of a tenement dwelling? | Pic 641: Do you agree with Ida Tarbell's perspectives on trusts?

_____

Quote 641: Lincoln Steffens' opinion of the Tammany Hall machine was: *a. positive   b. negative*

Note the topic the following muckrakers took on in their publications and how strongly you personally feel about the issue on a 1-3 scale (1=not important, 2=interesting, 3=important to me)

Muckraker	Issue	My rating
Lincoln Steffens		
Ida Tarbell		
Thomas Lawson		
David G. Phillips		
Ray S. Baker		
John Spargo		
Harvey Wiley		

'White slavery'

'Americanize'

Thinking Globally 642 – How does this article **summarize** *the views of Karl Marx and F. Engels?*

In "Why is there no Socialism in the United States," what answers did Werner Sombart give?

1)   2)

3)   4)

Initiative

Referendum

Recall

Pic 644: The message the pacifists had was:

| Quote 645: How did the first wave feminists describe their objectives?

Suffragist

Red light district

Muller v. Oregon

Louis Brandeis

Lochner v. New York

WCTU

Pic 646: What happened at the Triangle Shirtwaist Company that sparked outrage?

| Pic 647: What exactly is the meaning of this ad?

'Square Deal'

Examining the Evidence 648: What do you think about the evidence provided in the Muller case?

Elkins Act

Hepburn Act

Trusts

How did people differentiate 'good' v. 'bad' trusts?

| Pic 649: What message does this cartoon have regarding TR and trusts?

| Aside from TR, who else was a great trustbuster?

The Jungle

Meat Inspection Act

Pure Food and Drug Act

Pic 650: Okay 1-10 scale, how much would you like a job inspecting meat in a slaughterhouse? | Quote 651: Why is this statement by TR called 'prophetic'?

Note the milestones in conservation starting with the Desert Act: | Pic 651: Where are TR and John Muir in this pic?

_____

| Where is their selfie-stick?

Pg. 652: What are some of the things The Environmentalists did to become 'Makers of America'?

_____

_____

_____

Pic 654: How did these loggers contribute to the term *skid row*? | Pic 654 (bot.): Why did Muir say, "Damn Hetch Hetchy?"

John Muir

Gifford Pinchot

"Roosevelt Panic" of 1907

Pic 655: These people are said to be foreshadowing what exactly? | Pic 656: What did TR do in the election of 1908 and after it- that is to say, what is his legacy?

Dollar diplomacy

What do the authors mean by saying Taft was a 'round peg in a square hole?'

| Pic 657: What is TR looking at here exactly?

Payne-Aldrich Bill

'New Nationalism'

Bull Moose Party

New Freedom

What was Herbert Croly basic thesis in the *Promise of American Life*?

| Pic 660: Find a symbol in this cartoon and what it means:

Do you agree with his thesis?

Map 660: While Wilson won the South, name three states that the Bull Moose won:

1)   2)   3)

Varying Viewpoints 661: How did the following define and characterize Progressives?

Richard Hofstadter   *Gabriel Kolko*   *Wiebe & Hays*

Muncy, Gordon & Skocpol   *Daniel Rodgers*

"This is the war to end all wars- that will make the world safe for democracy" –Woodrow Wilson (Worst prediction of the century)

Quote 663: Wilson believes in this statement that: *a. laissez-faire is good   b. regulation is good*

Underwood Tariff _____

Pic 664: How does this artwork portray Wilson?

_____

Federal Reserve Act _____

'Federal Reserve Notes' _____

Federal Trade Commission Act _____

Clayton Anti-Trust Act _____

Holding companies _____

Workingmen's Compensation Act _____

Adamson Act _____

Jones Act _____

Pic 666: Who is in Haiti in this picture and what are they doing there?	In general, why, according to the evidence on this map, did Latin Americans accuse the U.S. of turning the Caribbean into a 'Yankee Lake?'

Mexican Revolution _____

Victoriano Huerta _____

Tampico Incident _____

Pic 668: Describe what is happening on this image:	Pic 668 (bot.): How did most Americans feel about Pancho Villa and why?

'Black Jack' John J. Pershing _____

Describe the 'chain reaction' that went down in Europe in 1914 to spark WWI:

Central Powers

Allied Powers

Chart 669: Did more Americans have blood ties to the Central Powers or the Allies?

Chart 670: Which side did the U.S. export more to in this war?

Quote 670: This message is one of _____ from the German-American community.

     a. support   *b. protest*

Map 670: Was the *Lusitania* sunk inside or outside the declared warzone?

U-boats

Lusitania

Pic 671: What was U-boat short for in German?

| Image 671 (right): After reading the NOTICE!
| on this, would you have taken the *Lusitania*?
|
|

Pic 672: Is this a propaganda piece? How do?

| What did the German command want in
| exchange for not sinking merchant ships
| regarding the British blockade of Germany?
|
|
|

Charles Evans Hughes

"He Kept Us Out of War"

Map 673: Which parts of the country tended to vote against Wilson?

| Why did Germany change policy and issue the warning
| to the Allies that *all* ships were now targets?
|
|
|

Zimmerman Telegram

Pic 674: Why did Wilson ask Congress for the authority to issue a War Declaration instead of just do it himself?	Quote 674: Note three words in this Wilson statement that indicate 'idealism'

Wilsonian idealism

Self-determination

Fourteen Points

Pic 675: What about this message is anti-German propaganda?	Note some anti-German nicknames and other labels that circulated in this era:

Committee on Public Information

Pic 676: This poster is _____ *a. offering money* *b. running a guilt trip*	What message did the song *Over There* convey?

Espionage Act

Schenck v. USA

War Industries Board

'Victory gardens'

Pic 678 (top): What kinds of jobs did women take during WWI?	Pic 678 (bot.): Why are these steel workers in Pittsburgh being beaten?	How were German-related things treated in the U.S.? Give three examples: 1) 2) 3)

Industrial Workers of the World

Wobblies

Great Migration

Pic 679: What happened in Chicago in 1919 and why?

Contending Voices 679 - Summarize the views of the following:

Carrie Chapman Catt   *Mrs. Barclay Hazard*

With whom do you agree more?

Nineteenth Amendment

Maternity Act

What does the term 'making Playboys into Doughboys' mean?

Table 680: List the countries in which women achieved voting rights during the following times:

Before 1918:

In 1918:

1919-1920:

1924-1946:

1947-1952:

1956-1974:

After 1974:

AEF

Quote 681: How did John Dos Passos feel about going to war? | Pic 681: Does this picture 'agree' or 'disagree' with John Dos Passos? Why?

Bolsheviks

The song *Mademoiselle from Armentieres* is saying something about French girls, what is it? | Pic 682: This post is asking soldiers to do what, exactly?

Map 682: Of the six major Allied victories and deadlocked battles, note them in chronological order:

1)   2)   3)

4)   5)   6)

Chateau-Thierry

Pg. 683: Examining the Evidence. What about American history does this item illuminate?

Meuse-Argonne offensive

Pic 684: What horrors of trench war does this image depict? | Chart 684: Copy the bar graph:
| Russia
| Germany
| France
| British
| Austria
| Italy
| USA

Note three reasons the Germans starting coming out of the trenches saying *Kamerad* just before the Americans were in danger of running out of supplies:

1)   2)   3)

Influenza

Pic 685: What was a 'Gold Star Mother'? | Did black American soldiers fight in the war too?

What does the term 'Wilson steps down from Olympus' mean in the context of the end of the war?

Quote 686: H.G. Wells (who perhaps ironically wrote *War of the Worlds*) was a _____ of the League of Nations and President Wilson's idealistic vision:

　　　　　　　　　　　　　　　　　　　　　　a. proponent　　　　*b. opponent*

League of Nations

Big Four

David Lloyd George

Georges Clemenceau

What did Clemenceau demand for the Rhineland and Saar Valley? | Why were the Italians angry about Fiume? | What did China get during the negotiation?

Treaty of Versailles

The treaty, according to the authors, was based on　　　*a. vengeance*　　*b. reconciliation*

Irreconcilables

Pic 687: Is this cartoon's POV pro or anti-ratification? | What was the conclusion of the 'Solemn Referendum' of 1920?

Varying Viewpoints 689: How did each historian argue on the question of Wilson's idealism?

George Kennan & Henry Kissinger　　　　　　*Arthur Link & Thomas Knock*

W.A. Williams　　　　　*J.M. Cooper*　　　　　*Erez Manela*

Hey, psst? What's the secret code to get into the Great Gatsby party?

Quote 692: What does America need now, according to Harding?	What are some things Americans did to begin a decade of 'homegrown prosperity?'

Bolshevik Revolution

The Red Scare

Syndicalism laws

American plan

What happened in the Sacco and Vanzetti case?	Pic 693: Who claimed responsibility for this terrorist-style act on Wall Street?

Pic 694: Do you believe the KKK should have the same right to free speech and assembly as any other group? Why or why not?	Quote 694: Which of the things cited by Hiram Evans as having been lost by the Nordic (Anglo-Saxon) Americans in his generation are cited as being contentious issues still today?

Note the names of two KKK songs sung during 'konclaves' in front of the fiery cross:	Pic 695: Do you agree with the cartoonist here that only U.S. control of mass immigration will stop an otherwise unlimited flow?

'100% American'

Immigration Act of 1924

What were the specific overall goals of the 1924 Immigration Act?	What was the reaction in Japan to the termination of immigration from there?

What alternative visions to the Immigration Act did Horace Kallen and Randolph Bourne propose?

    Kallen: *Bourne:*

Today 1,000,000 people per year are allowed to immigrate legally to the USA. Another million enter illegally each year, but taking legal immigrants only, the total amounts to 2,740 per day. How many of the following would it take to fill the 1924 Immigration Act's quota of 150,000 *total* immigrants per year at the present rate?

                                        Days: Weeks: Months:

Cultural pluralism

Graph 696: What was the national origins quota system and how long did it last?

Eighteenth Amendment

Volstead Act

Pic 697: Why are these G-men happy? | Do you agree with the authors that it was naïve to
                                                        | believe America could successfully outlaw alcohol?
                                                        |
                                                        |
                                                        |
                                                        |

Quote 697: How did Henry Ford feel about the prohibition of alcoholic beverages?

Pg. 698: What are some of the things the Poles did to become 'Makers of America'?

Speakeasy

Rumrunner

What effects did Prohibition have on the following:

    Bank savings   *Absenteeism at work*   *Death rates and liver cirrhosis*

Gangsterism

Racketeering

Pic 700: Where do you think the line between 'businessman' and 'racketeer' is, and did Al Capone cross it?

Lindbergh law

John Dewey

'Bible Belt'

Scopes 'Monkey Trial'

Pic 701: Do you agree with this anti-evolution group or with biology teacher John Scopes? _____

How would you argue if you were the following lawyers, no matter which side you agree with?

William Jennings Bryan   *Clarence Darrow*

Fundamentalism

'Horseless chariot'

What influence on public life did the following have:

Automobile   *Advertising*   *Sports*   *Credit*

Pic 702: Was Babe Ruth a right or left-handed batter? | Pic 703: If you went up to this guy in 1896 and told him he would be the 'Father of the Traffic Jam,' how do you think he would react?

Henry Ford

Ransom E. Olds

Frederick W. Taylor

Detroit _____

Scientific Management _____

Fordism _____

How much did a new Ford cost around 1925? _____. Now go online and search: *inflation adjuster.* Input the amount in dollars, and see how much that much in 1925 is in today's money, inflation being what it has been lately. Would you buy a new car at that price?

Chart 704 (top): Ask your teacher or your mom how much they take home in one month of pay from work. Then, see if three months of their wage would buy them a new car today, as it did the average workingman after 1920. What did you find?

Chart 704 (bot.): What is the only five-year timeframe when the total number of cars in the U.S. went down?	Why do you think that is?	Pic 705: What is the motto of this early gas station?	Pic 705 (bot.): How did Ford reach out to women here?

Ford's first car came out in 1896. What year did the 1,000,000th American die in a car accident?	What was the 'Miracle at Kitty Hawk?'

Wright Brothers _____

Pic 706: What did Charles A. Lindbergh do at age 25 that electrified the world and made him a media sensation?

Spirit of St. Louis _____

Pic 707: If someone in your family called everyone into the living room and said, "Okay gang, let's sit for the next hour together and watch the radio," how would you react?	Quote 707: How would Will Hays the Movie Czar react if he saw some of the films made today?

'Nickelodeon' _____

Note the year and importance of the following early movies:

The Great Train Robbery   *Birth of a Nation*   *The Jazz Singer*

Margaret Sanger

Pic 708: How did Ms. Sanger employ creativity to get around the anti-free speech law prohibiting her from talking about birth control to audiences?

_____

| The flappers of the 1920s were _____
| than their parents of the Edwardian Age.
|
| *a. less inhibited   b. more serious*

Pg. 709: Examining the Evidence. What about American history did this movie illuminate?

_____

_____

_____

Pic 710 (top): Hold up, these are the 'renegade' flappers? How wild does their dress look to you on a 1-10 scale?

| Pic 710 (bot.): Alright, if some guy came up to you at the
| entrance to the beach and tried to measure your leg to see
| if too much was showing, what would you do?
|
|
|
|

Contending Voices 710 - Summarize the views of the following:

Henry Van Dyke

Duke Ellington
|
|
|
|
|
|

With whom do you agree more?

What kind of music might inspire debate like this today?

_____

UNIA

'Lost Generation'

Pic 711 (top): Marcus Garvey goal was:

| Pic 711 (bot.): Geographically speaking, where are the
| cultural hearths of jazz?
|

Modernism

'Lost Generation'

F. Scott Fitzgerald

Quote 712: In a veiled way, Mencken is describing William J. Bryan's followers as

    a. smart   *b. ignorant*

| Pic 712: What themes did Fitzgerald explore in his books?

What themes did the following explore in their literary works:

Ernest Hemingway   *Gertrude Stein*   *T.S. Eliot*   *Ezra Pound*

Robert Frost   *Carl Sandburg*   *Sherwood Anderson*

William Faulkner   *Kern and Hammerstein*   *Eugene O'Neill*

Thinking Globally 714 – When Virginia Woolf said "today the human character changed," she meant the old Victorian morality was being challenged not only by flappers and jazz but by high art as well. While reading, list the names of the concepts the modernist art, music, literature and building styles of the age reflected:

        Concept   *Specific title of work*

Harlem Renaissance

'New Negro'

Quote 716: Hughes found   *a. obstacles*   *b. inspiration*   in Harlem, New York.

Asterisk 716 (bot. of page): Looks like the textbook authors went to   *a. a lot*   *b. a little* trouble to secure the rights to use the Langston Hughes quote.

Langston Hughes

If you have gum in school, even if you shouldn't, go ahead and blow a bubble till it pops, and say, "That was the whole chapter in miniature."

Quote 720: President Hoover was   *a. optimistic*   *b. pessimistic*   about the future.

Characterize President Harding: | Characterize the 'good' and 'bad' guys in his Cabinet:

Exterior   *Interior* | 'Good'   'Bad'

'Old Guard'

Adkins v. Children's Hospital

Quote 721: What was Oliver Wendell Holmes' view | Pic 721: What is funny about this satire?
on the Nineteenth Amendment?

Pic 723: America's message to Europe was   *a. we're isolationist*   *b. how can we help?*

What did Charles Evans Hughes propose at the Disarmament Conference? | How did the
                                                                          | Japanese like it?

Nine-Power Treaty

Kellogg-Briand Pact

Ford-McCumber Tariff

Teapot Dome Scandal

Albert B. Fall

'Silent Cal'

McNary-Haugen Bill

Pic 726: This was all the bragging Calvin Coolidge ever did. At a dinner party, a woman bet him she could get him to say more than three words, and he replied:

a. "Oh, I know I have a reputation for modesty. It's false I assure you."   *b. "You lose."*

Pic 727: A 1930 tractor can be described as: *a. OMG!*   *b. totally awesome*   *c. both*

Map 728: Name a state in which the candidate won the majority of counties:

Coolidge _____   *Davis* _____   *La Follette* _____

Dawes Plan _____

Chart 729: It's worth it for how insane this was. Reproduce and label the entire debt cycle:

_____

Herbert Hoover _____

Al Smith _____

Pic 730: You know it's hyperinflation has hit when people start burning _____ because they are cold at home. *a. firewood* *b. paper money*	Pic 731: Hoover started the trend perfected by modern candidates like Donald Trump, who in 2016 had up to five rallies per day in front of thousands of people. Why was it called 'whistle stopping' then?

Agricultural Marketing Act _____

Smoot-Hawley Tariff _____

Contending Voices 732 - Summarize the views of the following:

Willis Hawley   *New York Times Economists*

With whom do you agree more?

_____

Black Tuesday _____

Pic 733: Would you buy this car for $100? _____

Chart 733: Copy the Index of Common Stock Prices:

```
200
180
160
140
120
100
 80
 60
 40
 20
  0
      1921  1923  1925  1927  1929  1931  1933  1935  1937  1939
```

Quote 734: What did the writer mean when he said the U.S. was in poverty in the midst of plenty?

_____

Hooverville

Quotes 736 (right): What did Hoover believe should *not* be done by the government because it would go against the spirit of the national fiber of rugged individualism?

Today, over 100,000,000 million people in America are dependent on public assistance, which is nearly the entire population of the country in 1930. But there are no soup lines like in Pic 736. Why not?

_____

Pic 739: What did the Bonus Army want in this pic?

Pg. 737: Examining the Evidence. What about American history does this item illuminate?

_____

_____

_____

RFC

Norris-La Guardia Act

Bonus Army

Pic 740: What did the Japanese
do to China in the mid-1930s?

_____

Sounds like a soap opera, but we're starting a new club, called the Popular History Front, and building a Hooverville behind the school. Want in? "Okie."

Quote 751: What did FDR appeal to within Americans to get the country's economy back on track?

_____

Franklin D. Roosevelt
_____

Eleanor Roosevelt
_____

Pic 743: Why did FDR call Eleanor "his legs?"

| Quote 743: FDR believe the government has no role to play but diplomacy and national defense.

| *a. True*   *b. False*
_____

Brain Trust
_____

New Deal
_____

Pic 744: Why wasn't this cover published when the actual magazine came out in March, 1933?

| What were FDR's 'Three Rs?'
_____

Pic 745: What does this man holding the sign want?

_____

What was undertaken during the *Hundred Days*?

| Quote 745: Do you think what this
| Chinese visitor to America says is still
| true? Why or why not?
_____

Chart 746: Without skipping lines, note the early legislative actions of the New Deal's Three Rs:

RECOVERY   *RELIEF*   *REFORM*

Pic 747: What do the authors claim FDR was 'ingenious' at?

_____

Glass-Steagall Act _____

FDIC _____

CCC _____

Pic 748: Remember the Tlingit from Ch. 1? The Native Alaskans? What are they doing here?

_____

Harry Hopkins _____

Chart 749: Without skipping lines, note the later legislative actions of the New Deal's Three Rs:

RECOVERY   *RELIEF*   *REFORM*

_____

AAA _____

Father Coughlin _____

Francis Townsend _____

Huey Long _____

Quote 750: Father Coughlin   *a. advocated*   *b. fought against*   American intervention in multinational organizations.

Based on this information, Coughlin would likely be   *a. for*   *b. against*   the U.S. going into WWII.

Gerald L.K. Smith _____

Federal Art Project

How did the following women contribute to the national discussion?

Frances Perkins　　*Mary M. Bethune*　　*Ruth Benedict*　　*Margaret Mead*　　*Pearl Buck*

Of these contributors, who would you most like to have lunch with to and talk about their subject?

NRA

Pic 753: What is Bethune trying to do here?	Pic 754: Describe the awesome power of the Grand Coulee Dam:

Dust Bowl

Pic 755: What were 'Okies' and 'Arkies'?	What kinds of themes did John Steinbeck explore in his works?

Map 756: Which states were most affected by the dust?	What caused it?	Btw did you get the Lady Godiva reference? Do an image search on her if you didn't... but only if your teacher says it's okay...

TVA

Map 757: For each state, note the number of power plants and the names of cities serviced by TVA:

	Number of plants	*Cities*
Mississippi		
Alabama		
Georgia		
Kentucky		
North Carolina		
Tennessee		

Chart 758: Randomly going back in time to an American house, what are the chances the house you wind up visiting has power in the following years:

1900:	1910:	1920:	1930:	1940:	1950:	1960:

Social Security Act

Wagner Act

Flint Sit Down Strike

Fair Labor Standards Act

Quote 759: What is the essential message of this auto worker? | Pic 759: Why doesn't GM fire these workers?

Chart 760: In 1936 (where the indicator touches the green line), how many industrialized countries had fewer union workers than the U.S.?

Which country has the highest percentage today?

_____

Which is below the U.S. today? _____

Twentieth Amendment

Contending Voices 761 – How did each think about the New Deal at its zenith:

   FDR   _Herbert Hoover_

Court-packing plan

Keynesianism

Varying Viewpoints 766: Note the perspectives of the following historians on the New Deal:

A. Schlesinger   _Carl Degler_   _Barton Bernstein_   _Alan Brinkley_

David Kennedy   _Kessler-Harris, Gordon & Mettler_   _William Leuchtenburg_

And now may I present to you: The New Deal! "Ooo, ahh... amazing! What will it do?" I don't know but it's new and I want on that dime!

Quote 769: When FDR spoke of quarantine here, he was most likely meaning to isolate:

    a. patients with contagious diseases   *b. world leaders he viewed as extremists*

London Economic Conference
_____

Cordell Hull
_____

Tydings-McDuffie Act
_____

Why were some Christians upset that FDR recognized the Soviet government which ruled Russia?

_____

Good Neighbor Policy
_____

Pic 770: FDR   *a. believed American dominance was better*   *b. looked for hemisphere-wide unity*

Reciprocal Trade Agreements
_____

How do the authors colorfully describe the following dictators:

    Joseph Stalin   *Benito Mussolini*   *Adolf Hitler*

_____

Rome-Berlin Axis
_____

Pic 772 (left): The overarching theme of this rally is: *a. liberalism* *b. national unity*	Pic 772 (right): What did this poster argue Hitler was the last home from for the German?

Tripartite Act
_____

Johnson Debt Default Act
_____

Gerald Nye
_____

In 1935 the most decorated soldier in American history, Maj. Gen. Smedley Butler, released a book called *War is a Racket*. It shocked the country and increased public demand for an investigation into why the U.S. really went into WWI and got involved in so many international 'entanglements' in Europe and Latin America. Senator Nye was selected to investigate, and his commission found out some unsettling things. What were they?

Neutrality Acts

Quote 773: Lagging in colonial holdings, Mussolini conquered this African country: _____

Pic 773: In this cartoon, what is America? _____

While some Americans believed the Spanish Loyalists were pro-democratic reformers, others believed they were _____ because the Soviets helped them.

a. communist stooges   *b. seeking to restore the empire*

| Quote 774: Why did this person
| join the Lincoln Brigade?
|
|
|_____

Abraham Lincoln Brigade

Was the American government under FDR truly neutral in the Japanese-Chinese conflict of 1937?

Quarantine Speech

Contrast the sinking of the *Panay* in 1937 with the sinking of the *Maine* in 1898:

| How did the Japanese treat American whites
| in occupied China?
|
|
|
|

Appeasement

Hitler-Stalin Pact

Place the following actions by the German government into the correct chronological order: *Anschluss with Austria, Absorption of Czechoslovakia, Munich Conference, Invasion of Poland, Militarization of the Rhineland, Annexation of the Sudetenland:*

1)   2)   3)

4)   5)   6)

Pic 775: The world's most stigmatized symbol, the *Hakenkreuz*, shown here dredging its way through Poland, is generally translated into English as:

a. Hooked Cross   b. Gammadion   c. Swastika

Quote 776: If the German attack on Poland began at dawn on Sept. 1, 1939 and by mid-afternoon *Luftwaffe* planes were flying over the Polish capital, why did Roosevelt get this call in the middle of the night?

| Quote 776 (bot): Hitler argued this was
| a war to ____ of the German people.
|
| *a. increase the wealth*
|
| *b. secure the existence*
|

Lebensraum

Neutrality Act of 1939

"Phony War"

What happened in the Polish Campaign?	Who attacked Finland and what happened?

Winston Churchill

Contending Voices 777 - Summarize the views of the following:

Sterling Morton	FDR

With whom do you agree more?

Pic 777: Calling it the greatest moment of his life, Hitler is seen here doing what, where?	What did the conscription law of 1940 do?

Pg. 778: Examining the Evidence. What about American neutrality does this item illuminate?

Havana Conference

Pogroms

Josef Goebbels

Kristallnacht

Pic 779: Jewish emigration from Germany was encouraged via the Haavara Transfer Agreement (1933), whereby Jews deposited money into an account in Germany where it was used to buy tools and equipment needed to build a new Jewish state in Palestine, migrated to Palestine, then got the money back from a bank in Tel-Aviv run by a Jewish company after the tools had been sold to previous settlers. Ten percent of Germany's Jews migrated under the Transfer Agreement, to the point where Tel Aviv came to be the world's foremost example of a Bauhaus city, built in a modernist architectural style brought from Europe by the new arrivals. But many Jews did not migrate, until the fateful voyage of the *St. Louis.* What happened to it?

War Refugee Board

Pic 780: This Jewish refugee, who helped the U.S. develop the atomic bomb during WWII, was:	The Battle of Britain was fought a. on land b. in the sea c. in the air
Along with Henry Ford, Walt Disney and William Randolph Hearst, this famous aviator advocated the 'Fortress America' concept:	Pic 781: The isolationists would have _____ with the message of this propaganda poster. a. agreed b. disagreed

Robert A. Taft

Lend-Lease Bill

"Send guns, not sons"

"Arsenal of democracy"

Wilson's campaign slogan in 1916 was "He kept us out of war," while Roosevelt's in 1940 was, "Your boys are not going to be sent into any foreign wars." To what extent do you think Roosevelt assumed the U.S. would eventually be in WWII?	Map 782: Who did your state vote for in 1940?
Pic 783: Were these mothers justified in their fear? Why or why not?	Map 783: Name the places the 'neutral' U.S. sent war material:

Robin Moor

Atlantic Charter

Pic 784: What happened in June, 1940 to change the situation for Britain and U.S. fear that it would be defeated by Hitler?

Quote 784: Harry Truman was partial to:

    a. Stalin   *b. Hitler*   *c. neither*

Describe the reasons for and situation behind the clashes involving the following:

Greer   *Kearney*   *Reuben James*

"China Incident"

Describe the 'two painful alternatives' facing Japan in late-1941:

1)   *2)*

If you were a lawyer arguing both sides of the case, what would your main points be?

FDR and the government knew about Pearl Harbor in advance and were negligent	*Pearl Harbor was a total surprise and no one could have known*

Pearl Harbor

Pic 786: Describe the damage done by the Japanese in detail both in physical damage and in dealing a great strategic blow to the Americans:

Quote 789: Brainstorm some some things ordinary Americans would be asked to do, and to give up, so that FDR's admonishment made in this quote could come to fruition:

ABC-1 Agreement

What were some reasons that 'time was on America's side?'	What does 'decadent' mean in the context of 'going soft?'

Pic 790: How many Americans would serve in the U.S. military during WWII? _____

Quote 790: Note some songs sung after Pearl Harbor that are here called here nationalistic and racist by the authors:

Executive Order 9066

Pic 791: Selected suspension of citizen rights is something that happens in some wars, in some countries, depending on law, and what that country's leadership thinks is prudent during wartime. The latest research shows 36,000 noncitizen Japanese (enemy aliens) were interned, as well as 14,000 Germans and Italians. To this number, however, were added 71,000 Japanese-Americans (citizens) who were brought to relocation centers, in a suspension of *habeas corpus*. Was this necessary in your opinion for either of the groups? When, if ever, should regular legal processes be set-aside during wartime for the following:

"ENEMY ALIENS"	CITIZENS OF "ENEMY" DESCENT

Korematsu v. U.S.

What were the following put in charge of?

WPB   *OPA*   *NWLB*

Pg. 792: What are some of the things the Japanese did to become 'Makers of America?'

Smith-Connally Anti-Strike Act

How did the following organize women in the war effort?

WACs   *WAVES*   *SPARs*   *WOW (Pic 795)*

***Bracero* program**

Map 796: From most to least, note the regions people migrated from and to during WWII:

1)

2)

3)

4)

5)

6)

How did the following help in the war effort?

FEPC   *CORE*   *Migration of African-Americans*

'Code talkers'

Zoot-suit riot

Detroit Riot

Pic 797: What role did the Tuskegee Airmen have in WWII?

Contending Voices 797 - Summarize the views of the following:

FDR	*African-American soldier*

With whom do you agree more?

| Pic 798: What made the code talkers so successful at 'getting the message across'? | Pic 798 (right): This man believes it should be illegal to discriminate in hiring- but for what reason? |

Office of Scientific Research

Describe the costs of WWII in comparison with past wars:	Graph 799: The 2016 debt rang up at 19 trillion dollars. If that were on this graph, the length of the bar would be approximately:
	a. double b. the height of a basketball hoop

"Welfare-warfare state"

Note some of the conquests Japan had in the Pacific in late-1941 and 1942:

Douglas MacArthur

Bataan Death March

Corregidor

| Map 800: Bataan and Corregidor are in this country: | Pic 800: What is historic about this particular picture? |

Battle of Midway _____

Battle of the Coral Sea _____

Alcan Highway _____

Guadalcanal _____

'Leapfrogging' _____

Chester Nimitz _____

Map 801: Note the timeframes for the following battles

_____ _Pearl Harbor_   _____ _Coral Sea_   _____ _Midway_

_____ _Guadalcanal_   _____ _Tarawa_   _____ _Saipan_

_____ _Philippines Sea_   _____ _Guam_   _____ _Leyte Gulf_

_____ _Iwo Jima_   _____ _Okinawa_   _____ _Hiroshima_

'Turkey Shoot' _____

'Suicide Cliff' _____

'Wolf Pack' _____

Battle of the Atlantic _____

"The Desert Fox" _____

Bernard Montgomery _____

El Alamein _____

Stalingrad _____

"Soft underbelly" _____

Quote 802: What did Churchill say about the Germans? | Pic 803: Where are these women going?

'Unconditional surrender' _____

Monte Cassino _____

D-Day _____

Tehran Conference _____

Normandy _____

Iron Ring _____

George Patton _____

French 'underground' _____

Pic 804: Describe the relationship between Churchill and Roosevelt:	Map 805 Note the dates of the following events:
	_____ *Germans repulsed from Moscow*
	_____ *Battle of Stalingrad* _____ *Battle of El Alamein*
	_____ *Kasserine Pass* _____ *Siege of Leningrad*
Pic 806: D-Day is described as 'amphibious,' why?	_____ *Rome Liberated* _____ *D-Day*
	_____ *Battle of the Bulge* _____ *German Surrender*

Harry S. Truman _____

Thomas E. Dewey _____

Note some reasons FDR defeated Dewey in the 1944 election:

_____

'Blockbuster' _____

Pic 807: This hand-clasping photo-op between Russian and American comrades was the highpoint of American and Soviet relations. How were the American and Soviet visions of the postwar order different?

_____

Map 807: What town in Belgium was the 'Bulge' the center of?

Pg. 808: Examining the Evidence. What about American history does this document illuminate?

Pic 809: Why is this German woman brought by the Allies to this prison camp looking away?

V-E Day

'The silent service'

'I have returned'

Battle of Leyte Gulf

Kamikaze

Potsdam Conference

Albert Einstein

Manhattan Project

Hiroshima

Pic 810: Where was this iconic picture taken?
| Pic 811: Note the death toll of the atomic bombing of Hiroshima:
|
| _Instantly:_ _____   _Later on:_ _____
|

Quote 811: What did atom bomb designer Robert Oppenheimer say about himself after seeing it work?
| Chart 813: The best place to be a civilian
| in WWII was:
|
|

Pic 814 (top): The Japanese surrender was signed aboard _____

V-J Day

Varying Viewpoints 815: What did the following historians say about the atomic bombing of Japan?

Gar Alperovitz   _Richard Rhodes_   _Sherwin, Bernstein et al._   _RJC Butow_   _Your opinion_

Better dead than red. Till you realize most of them actually hate their government just like we do. Then you just feel sorry for everyone.

Quote 820: What do you think Churchill meant when he said this?	Describe Truman's personality:

Yalta Conference

Pic 821: Which of the Big Three was not fated to see the end of the war? _____

What did it mean that Poland and other Eastern European countries were 'sold out' at Yalta?

'Sphere of influence'

Map 822: This is cartographic propaganda, which portrays, whether true or false, a map that 'says something' to the viewer. What does this huge red area of Eurasia with its satellite states make you *feel* like?	Contrast Stalin's vision of a world of 'spheres of influences' against FDR's Wilsonian ideals:

Cold War

Bretton Woods Conf.

GATT

United Nations

Quote 823: Baruch believed atomic energy was: *a. great*   *b. dangerous*   *c. potentially both*

Nuremberg Trials

Pic 824: Why did some commentators and legal critics condemn the Nuremberg Trials?

Occupation zone

Satellite state

Quote 825: What did Churchill say has descended across Europe? _____

Map 825: What happened to the following Third Reich territories?

   East Prussia: Austria:

   Berlin: Bavaria:

Containment doctrine

Truman Doctrine

Marshall Plan

Pic 826: Why were these people grateful | Pic 827: This cartoonist is saying U.S. foreign
upon seeing the plane shown here? | policy is:
                                        |
                                        | *a. certain to be successful   b. uncertain*

Contending Voices 827 - Summarize the views of the following:

   George F. Kennan   *Henry A. Wallace*

With whom do you agree more?

Map 828: Where did most Marshall Plan aid go? | Pic 828: What is the message of this sign
                                              | beyond what it literally says?

Pic 829: What statement does this cartoon make | Pic 829 (bot.): What was the main goal of
about the motivations behind Marshall Plan aid? | NATO?

NATO

Describe some things that happened to shorten the American occupation of Japan:

Pic 830: Why would you want more than a bikini on while visiting South Pacific paradise Bikini Island in 1954?

Quote 831: Was Condon right to be worried about this?

Taiwan

Dean Acheson

H-bomb

NSC-68

Pg. 833: What are some of the things scientists and engineers have done to become 'Makers of America?'

Korean War

38th Parallel

Map 834: The river where Chinese troops came over into Korea to fight Americas is the:

Describe what happened to control over Korean territory in the four phases shown:

1)   2)

3)   4)

Pic 835: Why did Truman 'take heat' after firing MacArthur? _____

Loyalty Review Board

HUAC

Alger Hiss

Richard Nixon

The Rosenberg Trial

Pic 836: What is Senator McCarthy doing here?

As evidence has shown the Rosenbergs did in fact deliver atomic secrets to the Soviets, do you agree that they should have been executed for treason?

Joseph McCarthy

If a teacher in your school was outed as a communist, what would your position be on them?

a. they should be fired   *b. they should only be fired only if they bring their opinions into the classroom*   *c. they should be free to hold their opinions without fear of losing their job*

McCarthyism

Army-McCarthy Hearings

Reinhold Niebuhr

'The American Way'

E.O. 9981

Taft-Hartley Act

Operation Dixie

Employment Act of 1946

GI Bill

Pic 838: Do you think veterans should get preferential treatment getting into colleges and jobs? Why or why not? | Pic 839: Why was this such a | 'surprise?'

Fair Deal

Pic 840: Why is Truman so happy in this famous picture? | Quote 840 (right): Conservatives | generally _____ the New Deal. | | *a. liked*   *b. didn't like*

The Long Boom

Chart 841: Why do you think there was such a big increase in the national defense budget after the year 2000? | What year did the U.S. government spend the | most on defense as a percentage of the | entire federal budget?

Note some of the things that factored into the postwar prosperity era:

_____

Sunbelt
_____

Benjamin Spock
_____

Pic 842: Why did agribusiness gain so much over the traditional family farm during the late-20ᵗʰ century?	Map 843: Note the trends in where people were moving:
(Whatever you do, do *not* Youtube: *the Meatrix* to see agribusiness in action)	

Pg. 844: What are some of the things suburbanites have done to become 'Makers of America?'

_____

_____

_____

Suburb
_____

Levittown
_____

'White flight'
_____

'Wealth gap'
_____

Baby boom
_____

About what years defined the Baby boom era? _____

Varying Viewpoints 847: Summarize how each of the following argued on blame for the Cold War:

    Orthodox appraisal   *Revisionists*   *the Kolkos*   *Gladdis & Leffler*

_____

Quote 850: Eisenhower's message here is: *a. optimistic   b. positive   c. a warning   d. all of these*

IBM is a good company to think about when considering the miniaturization of technology in this era. What kinds of new devices appeared in America which helped increase affluence?

'White collar' _____

'Blue collar' _____

'Cult of domesticity' _____

Table 851: Looking at 2010 and 1960, state whether the relative number of women working in each of the five types of work has been going up or down:

White-collar	*Clerical*	*Manual*	*Farm*	*Service*

The Feminine Mystique _____

Pic 851: This computer was the size of a room. What size is it today? _____

'Fast food'-style _____

Summarize some developments in the following fields during the 1950s:

TV	*Movies*	*Religion*	*Sports*

Rock 'n' roll _____

Pg. 852: Examining the Evidence. What about American history does this ad illuminate?

_____

_____

_____

Graph 853: About _____% of homes had a TV in 1950, which went up to _____% by 1960.

_____

Pic 854 (top): The sector of the economy that went up most dramatically during this era was

a. agriculture   b. industry   c. service

As consumerism went up as an overall lifestyle, what happened to popular notions about sexuality?

| Pic 854 (bot.): What about this image symbolizes consumerism?

| Pic 855: What do the authors call Elvis the 'high priest' of?

How did the following books criticize consumerism as a lifestyle?

The Lonely Crowd   The Organization Man   The Affluent Society

'I like Ike'

Checkers Speech

Pic 855: As photo ops like this and the Checkers Speech testified, what kinds of things could savvy politicians do to increase their 'brand' in the mind of the public?

Map 856: Which states in general voted for Adlai Stevenson instead of the Eisenhower-Nixon ticket?

| Pic 856 & Quote 856: If the soldier and the African-American woman could switch places, do you think either of them would do it? Why or why not?

Pic 857: What kinds of segregated norms existed in the South?

Note some of the people who were activists or writers against the segregation system:

Sweatt v. Painter

What kinds of laws were struck down in the 1940s and 1950s that led people to believe the segregation system as a whole might be broken in the 1960s?

Pic 858: Why are the people in this picture taunting this African American girl on her way to school?

Pic 859: Why did Martin Luther King and his wife get arrested in this picture?

Brown v. Board of Ed.

Greensboro 'Sit in'

SNCC

Pg. 860: What are some of the things these African American migrants did to become 'Makers of America?'

Operation Wetback

Pic 862: With immigration the key issue in the 2016 presidential race, compare and contrast the Mexican government's position on the issue now versus then:

| Pic 863: Can you imagine cars with | bench seats comfortable enough like | couches that you'd actually *want* to sit | in it and watch a movie?

Drive-in

Federal Highway Act

John Foster Dulles

Policy of boldness

Nikita Khrushchev

Hungarian Uprising

Battle of Dien Bien Phu

Ho Chi Minh

'The Shah'

Suez crisis

Gemal Abdel Nasser

Pic 864: What effect on American communist sympathizers did these events in Budapest have?

| Pic 865: What effect on Eisenhower did the unilateral action in Suez have?

OPEC

Jimmy Hoffa

Sputnik I

Sputnik II

ICBM

'Rocket fever'

NASA

NDEA

U-2 incident

Fidel Castro

Kitchen debate

John F. Kennedy

Pic 867: The good looking Kennedys found out that media mattered a great deal in the age of television. How did the 1960 election demonstrate that?

Contending Voices 867 - Summarize the views of the following:

Richard Nixon   *Nikita Khrushchev*

Map 868: Was the electoral vote or popular vote closer between Kennedy and Nixon? | Which states voted for the third-party candidate Byrd?

Pg. 869: Examining the Evidence. What about American history does the shopping mall illuminate?

_____

_____

_____

Military-industrial complex

Abstract expressionism

Pic 870: Note the styles and contributions of the following artists, architects and writers:

Roy Lichtenstein   _Jackson Pollock_   _William de Kooning_

Mark Rothko   _Andy Warhol_   _Frank Lloyd Wright_

Louis Kahn   _I.M. Pei_   _Norman Mailer_

James Jones   _Joseph Heller_   _Kurt Vonnegut_

John Updike   _John Cheever_   _Gore Vidal_

Robert Lowell   _Sylvia Plath_   _Ernest Hemingway (Pic. 871)_

Tennessee Williams   *Arthur Miller*   *Alan Ginsberg (Quote 871)*

Edward Albee   *Lorraine Hansberry*   *J.D. Salinger*

Ralph Ellison   *Saul Bellow*   *Harper Lee*

Beat Generation (pg. 872)

Makers of America 872: What did the Beat Generation do to become 'Makers of America'?

Who were the new 'cultural voices' from underrepresented groups?	Who were the writers of the Southern Renaissance?	Note the famous Jewish writers of the time and their themes:

Bobby Kennedy

J. Edgar Hoover

Robert McNamara

'New Frontier'

Peace Corps

| Pic 875 (left): What did Neil Armstrong say as he became the first human being to walk on the Moon? | Pic 875 (right): Do you think when man walked on the Moon it was the greatest achievement in all of history? Why or why not? |

Apollo Program

Adjusted for inflation, the entire Apollo Program, consisting of all the research and development of products and equipment, all the training, and the six landings, cost 109 billion dollars. A mission to Mars program is estimated by NASA to cost about the same over ten years' time. The wars in the Middle East since Sept. 11th, on the other hand, have cost 1,700 billion dollars as of 2015. If America didn't have to deal with that, how many times could we have established a human presence on Mars? Do you think that would have been a better option? Why or why not?

Berlin Wall

EEC

Trade Expansion Act

Globalization

How did the doctrine of 'Massive Retaliation' differ from the doctrine of 'Flexible Response?'

| Pic 876: The Berlin Wall was built by the East German communists to:

a. keep people out   b. keep people in | Pic 876 (right): How long did the hated wall stand before guys like this one hammered it down in anger? |

Ngo Dinh Diem

Bay of Pigs invasion

Pic 877: Why did the Bay of Pigs invasion fail and how did it make the Kennedy Administration look?

Cuban Missile Crisis

What was revealed about this game of 'nuclear chicken' in 1991 with the opening of the Soviet archives?

| Ed. note: See the map on
| pg. 878? Totally bad
| placement. We will come
| back to it next chapter.

Détente

Freedom Riders

Pic 879: How do the authors describe the people who burned this bus? _____

Vote Education Project

Pic 880: How did these cops in Alabama control street protests?

| What happened at 'Ole Miss' when it was time
| for the school to be integrated by federal
| legislation?
|
|

March on Washington

Pic 881: What did Martin Luther King wish for people of all races in his 'I Have a Dream' speech?

| Quote 881: Kennedy implies in this
| statement that:
|
| *a. whites wouldn't trade their skin color*
|
| *b. whites would prefer to be black*
|

Nov. 22, 1963

Lyndon B. Johnson

Lee Harvey Oswald

Jack Ruby

Warren Commission

The CIA has been blamed for Kennedy's death, the international banking cartel has been blamed, the Soviets were looked at too, but the Warren Commission went with the 'lone nut who then amazingly got shot by another lone nut' conclusion. The jury is still out on this, at least informally. Maybe in your lifetime the records will be opened. In the meantime, do you think Kennedy was assassinated by a 'lone nut' or do you think it was a conspiracy of some kind?

Some say liberalism is the ideology of Western suicide. Others say it is our salvation. It can be one or the other, but it can't be both.

Quote 884: Whose windows were being shaken and who is doing the shaking in Dylan's lyric?	Note some of the things going on that changed American life in the stormy sixties:

The 'Johnson treatment'

Barack Obama famously gaffed by bestowing upon the Queen of England- 82-years-old at the time- an iPod during their first official meeting in 2009. Soon after, the Obamas gave British Prime Minister Gordon Brown a set of 25 DVDs containing movies he already had. Both of these were considered trash gifts bordering on insulting. By contrast, Brown got the Obamas a pen holder made from wood carved out of an anti-slave ship. How would you classify LBJ's gift to the pope?

Civil Rights Act

Affirmative Action

Do you agree with Johnson that Affirmative Action, the legal requirement that businesses above a certain size hire a certain percentage of nonwhite males and women, fulfills the ideal of 'equal opportunity'? Or do you agree with his opponents that equal opportunity should be based solely on merit and the decisions arrived at by the business owners themselves?

Great Society

Barry Goldwater

Pic 885: What emotion was Johnson appealing to by using this shock ad? _____

Gulf of Tonkin incident

Map 286: Where did Goldwater do well?	List some of the consequences of the following Great Society Programs:
	Poverty:
	Transportation:
	Arts:

Education:

Medicare:

Medicaid:

Immigration:

'Family unification':

'Head Start':

Desegregation:

24ᵗʰ Amendment

Freedom Summer

Mississippi Freedom Democratic party

Graph 888: On a whole, did the Great Society's 'War on Poverty' make much of a dent?	Pic 889: What happened at Selma, Alabama?

Voting Rights Act

Watts Riot

Black separatism

Malcolm X

Black Panther Party

Black Power

Contending Voices 890 - Summarize the views of the following:

Martin Luther King   *Malcolm X*

With whom do you agree more?

Marcus Garvey

What similarities did the Newark and Detroit riots share?

Viet Cong

Operation Rolling Thunder

What was Johnson's strategy and did it work?

| Why do the authors write, "The South
| Vietnamese were becoming spectators in
| their own war?
|
|
|

Six-Day War

What territories did Israel acquire in 1967 following the Six-Day War?

Antiwar demonstrations

Pic 892: The major handicap of the U.S. in the Vietnam war was a lack of:

a. technology   *b. national will to win*

| Pic 892 (bot.): What happened to this soldier
| in Vietnam?
|
|
|

"Hell no, we won't go!"

William Fulbright

"Doves"

Pic 893: What kinds of things did doves and other antiwar people find disturbing about the war in Viet Nam that they did not find 'wrong' about WWII or even WWI?

| LBJ dropped a metaphorical bomb on America
| on March 31, 1968. What was it and how did
| it serve to protect the status quo?
|
|
|
|
|

Tet Offensive

Hubert H. Humphrey

Was there a political motive behind the Arab American's murder of Robert Kennedy in 1968? | Pic 894: Why was all this extra security needed at the DNC in Chicago in 1968?

'Hawk'

Spiro Agnew

George Wallace

George Wallace was the last presidential contender in the history of the United States to run against the mandatory racial integration of the country.

What was his slogan? | *What did he do at the University of Alabama* | *What was his Vietnam stance?*

Map 895: What were the final stats in the hotly contested 1968 election?

Candidate	Electoral Votes	Popular Votes	Areas of U.S. won
Richard Nixon			
Hubert Humphrey			
George Wallace			

Many of the young people growing up in the late-1960s were angry about all authority. What do the things they were upset about mean to you- as in- how do you define these for yourself?

Racism   *Sexism*   *Imperialism*   *Oppression*

If you were growing up at this time, do you think you would have been rebellious? About what?

Thinking Globally 896: How did the following people and places contribute to the atmosphere of the '60s?

Herbert Marcuse, C. Wright Mills, Frantz Fanon & Jean-Paul Sartre   *Che, Ho, Lumumba & Mao*

Chinese Cultural Revolution   *The Prague Spring*   *Paris protests*

Tlatelolco Rally   *"Post-Materialist" concerns*   *Culture of repudiation of authority*

Hippies

Communes

Sexual Revolution

Stonewall Rebellion

SDS

Pic 898: What happened at UC Berkeley to make it a hotbed of the counterculture movement?	Pic 899: What city did the first gay rights march take place in and why?

What did the phrase 'the greening of America' mean (hint: not environmental!):

Vietnamization

Nixon Doctrine

'Silent majority'

My Lai massacre

Quote 900: What kinds of things about Vietnam demoralized this U.S. Marine?

Pic 900: Some consider this to be a poignant photograph while others consider it terrible. Others consider it other things. What do you consider it?

Kent State

Pic 901: What is the meaning of this cartoon's implication that for some people the 'Cold' War was 'Hot?' | Pic 901 (bot.): Why are these college students shocked?

Pentagon Papers

ABM

SALT

MIRVs

Pic 902: Why is this dinner so unique in the history of the Cold War? | Would you think America intervened if you were Chilean in this era? Why?

Pic 903: Note some of the cases and decisions that made many (like the people who made this sign) accuse the Supreme Court of 'judicial activism' above and beyond their intended powers:

Case   Controversial Decision

Miranda Warning

Food Stamps

SSI

AFDC

Philadelphia Plan

EPA

| Pic 904: Why did Racheal Carson's book *Silent Spring* help make her 'mother of the conservation movement'? | Pic 905: Would these Europeans tend to agree with the Hawks or the Doves? |

Earth Day

Clean Air Act

OSHA

CPSC

'Nanny state'

Why did Nixon take the U.S. dollar off the gold standard and what was the reaction?

Southern strategy

DMZ

George McGovern

Twenty-Third Amendment

| Map 878: On a separate paper, draw a free-hand map of Viet Nam and label the events. | How did the Vietnam War wind up? |

War Powers Act

Yom Kippur War

'Energy crisis'

| Pic 907: If you saw this sign at a gas station next time you went to get some gas, what would your reaction be? | Pic 907 (bot.): What does the Arab oil man want from this guy? |

Most American cars in the 1940s-1970s were:

a. small and fuel-efficient   *b. big and gas-guzzling*

International Energy Agency

Cadillac was always a symbol of the huge cars built by the Detroit automakers. In 1976, it came out with 'the last of the giants,' the Cadillac Fleetwood Brougham. Weighing in at over 5,200 pounds, it was 20 feet long, with "a hood long enough to serve as a pool table." The largest regular production car ever made, it was driven by an 8.2 liter, 500 cubic inch engine. In 1977, all GM, Ford and Chrysler cars, including the mighty Cadillac and the Lincoln Continental, were scaled down to compete with the foreign imports. What led U.S. automakers to start producing smaller cars at this point in history?

What is your favorite kind of car? Would you pay more in gas to get more luxury or room on the inside? Make a list of some of the things you would look for in your dream car:

Varying Viewpoints 908: What did the following historians argue about the Sixties?

Conservatives	Liberals	Van Deberg & P. Joseph
Jacquelyn Hall	Matusow & Schwarz	Charles Murray
Lawrence Meade	John Lewis Gaddis	Adam Garfinkle
Gitlin & Wells	William O'Neal	Kazin & Isserman
Sara Evans	McGirr & Perlstein	Rebecca Klatch

What do you want to do today? "Overturn the existing society dude." What do we replace it with? "I don't know, something groovy!"

Quote 911: What was President Ford's opinion in the State of the Nation address of 1975?

    a. optimistic   *b. pessimistic*

| Quote 911: What is Nixon claiming here?

Stagflation

Watergate scandal

In 2013, a scandal broke in which the Internal Revenue Service (IRS), which collects taxes and audits businesses and people it thinks are being dishonest on their tax forms, was accused of targeting Republicans and conservatives under the Obama Administration. Is there a precedent for this kind of accusation in U.S. history? State your case:

Gerald Ford

Pic 912 (top): What is going on in this comic?

| Pic 912 (bot.): What was contained in the
| 'Smoking Gun' tape that was so incriminating?

Pg. 913: Examining the Evidence. In your opinion, should taped White House discussions be public record, or do you agree with Nixon that presidents should have some privacy?

Pic 914: What is inflation in this context?

| Graph 914: Despite making an average of 50k
| instead of 5k as in 1960, why don't Americans
| 'feel' wealthier now- according to this chart?

Johnson is blamed for triggering the inflation by spending a lot of public money. What kinds of things did he spend it on?

| By spending on Middle East wars
| and record welfare state outlays
| simultaneously, Bush and Obama
| continued Johnson's pattern:
|
| *a. True*   *b. False*

Gerald Ford was bizarre as a president because he was:

a. Not the VP on the Nixon ticket   *b. Appointed by Congress*   *c. Both of these*

| What did Ford do that shocked the country regarding Nixon? | What did the Helsinki Accords, the diplomatic highlight of the Ford presidency, accomplish? |

Thinking Globally 916 – Summarize what the following people & items did to further globalization:

Woodrow Wilson   *Franklin Roosevelt*   *International Monetary Fund*

GATT   *WTO*   *UN*

Discuss some problems cited here brought about by the globalization process:

Pic 918: Why did Ford and Kissinger stop using the term détente?

Note the final costs of the Vietnam War after the U.S. pulled out in 1975:

Money spent: *Deaths:*   *Wounded:*

What else did America seem to have 'lost' in Vietnam aside from the physical costs?

ERA

| Pic 919: Before *Roe v. Wade* (1973), what was the law regarding abortions? | There have been over 50,000,000 abortions performed in America since *Roe v. Wade.* What do you think the law should be about it? |

Pg. 920: What are some of the things the Vietnamese have done to become 'Makers of America'?

_____

_____

_____

Pg. 922: What are some of the things Feminists have done to become 'Makers of America'?

_____

_____

_____

Pic 924: The three reasons Phyllis Schlafly cited for being against ERA were:

1)

2)   3)

Note the significance of the following cases:

Milliken v. Bradley:

Bakke case:

United States v. Wheeler:

Pic 925: Why did the whites shown here dislike the forced busing directives?

_____

New Right _____

Jimmy Carter _____

Pic 926: What did the following sides promise to do at the Camp David Accords?

    Israelis   *Palestinians*

_____

Under Carter, the fate of the Panama Canal was decided. What was it?

_____

'Oil shock' _____

Why is it that people on fixed incomes like the elderly, and people who put money in the bank to save it, get hurt financially when inflation is high (as it continued to be under Carter)?

Iranian Revolution

Malaise speech

Quote 927: Do you think Carter's words still hold true about the America you know today? Why or why not?

| Graph 928: Summarize the meaning of this graph: | What do you think will happen to prices in the future, say, five years from now? |

Pic 929: What was Milton Friedman's opinion of government management over the U.S. economy?

(Ask your teacher if you can get extra credit if you watch all 10 parts of *Free to Choose* on Youtube)

Contending Voices 930 - Summarize the views of the following:

Lewis Powell   *Douglas Fraser*

With whom do you agree more?

SALT II

Iran hostage crisis

Leonid Brezhnev

How did the 1980 Olympics illustrate Cold War tension?

It's morning in America. "Wait, don't hit snooze! Noooooooooooo!"

Quote 933: Which amendment of the Bill of Rights was Reagan promising to defend in this statement? (If you forgot them they are in the appendix on pg. A-14)

| The slogan of Reagan's campaign in
| 1980 was:
|
|

'Moral Majority'

On social issues like abortion, pornography, homosexuality, Feminism and hiring preferences for minority groups, Reagan:

| Note jobs Reagan had before
| president:
|
|_____

a. favored restriction   b. favored encouragement

Ted Kennedy

Chappaquiddick

Pic 934: Reagan cultivated an image of:

a. Youth   b. Down-home values   c. both

| Map 934: Reagans victory in 1980 was:
|
| *a. contested   b. a landslide*
|

Quote 935: Reagan made the following arguments to bolster the conservative case for prayer being allowed in schools again:

| Reagan was _____
| New Deal & Great Society-
| style programs:
|
| *a. for   b. against*
|

Margaret Thatcher

Pic 935: This was a major foreign policy success on Reagan's first day in office:

| Pic 936: Why is the right side of the White
| House connected to the U.S. Capitol building?
|
|

Prop. 13

Boll weevils

Supply-side economics

Yuppies

According to the Washington Post, the U.S. trade deficit for 2015 was over 484 billion dollars. Is this more or less than during the Reagan era?

SDI

Pic 937: Whether Reagan was bluffing or not, Star Wars totally demoralized the Soviet leadership. What is this comic trying to say about the reality of his statements?

Solidarity

Note the significance of the following:

Sanctions on USSR and Poland   *Downing of Korean airliner*

1984 Olympics in LA   *Beirut barracks attack*

Sandinistas   *'Contras'*

Granada   *1984 Election*

Perestroika

Glasnost

Map 939: The U.S. dealt weapons to _____ | The U.S. dealt weapons to _____ during the Reagan '80s:
Before the Reagan '80s: |
                                            | *a. Iraq   b. Iran   c. Somalia*
a. Iraq   b. Iran   c. Somalia |
                                            | The U.S. sold weapons to Saudi Arabia: *a. True b. False*
_____ was attacked |_____
by the Soviet Union in the 1980s.

INF Treaty

Iran-Contra Affair

Pic 941 (top): In a series of summit meetings, | Pic 941 (bot.): Why is this dude's hat hilarious?
Reagan met this Soviet leader: |
                                                 |
                                                 |
                                                 |
                                                 |

Map 940: Give a status update for each of the following during the 1980s:

Mexico:

Guatemala:

El Salvador:

Honduras:

Nicaragua:

Panama:

Colombia:

Venezuela:

Brazil:

Cuba:

Guantanamo:

Haiti:

Grenada:

Quote 942: Do you find this statement funny in any way? Why?

Jerry Falwell

To bolster the statement that the religious right and the New Left shared similar methods of getting their message across even though the message was different, the authors cite examples: Note these examples:

	New Left	*Christian Right*

Holding sessions:

Blocking entrances:

Chart 943: Has any president since Ford not grown the national debt? _____

The national debt in 1940 was very close to _____. The *rate* that the debt is growing seems to be

Check *U.S. Debt Clock* online. What is it today: | *a. rising   b. falling*   since Sept. 11, 2001.

Chart 944: Summarize this chart's findings:	Pic 944: Tell the story of when AIDS got to America and which groups were affected:

Sandra Day O'Connor

Note the significance of the following trials:

Ward's Cove Packing v. Antonia

Webster v. Reproductive Health Services

Planned Parenthood v. Casey

Pic 945: How does the cartoonist feel about Reagan having appointed a female S.C. justice?

Quote 946: What is Reagan's stance on abortion?	Quote 946 (bot.): What is Gordon Gecko's stance on greediness?

Black Monday

George H.W. Bush (41)

Pic 947 (top): How did Bush's campaign slogan in 1988 contrast with Reagan's hardline image?	Pic 947 (bot.): Would you stand in front of the tanks like this guy to achieve a political goal? If so, what would that goal be?

The following Soviet satellite states held free and multi-party elections in 1989:

Mikhail Gorbachev

Boris Yeltsin

Pic 948: How was Lenin an 'idol'?	Pic 948: One communist country erupted into civil war when it broke up. It was:

START II

Map 949: Note the events that took place in the following:

Poland:

East Germany:

Czechoslovakia:

Russia:

Chechnya:

Yugoslavia:

Kosovo:

Contending Voices 950 - Summarize the views of the following:

    Margaret Thatcher   *Mikhail Gorbachev*

With whom do you agree more?

Ethnic cleansing

Since the end of the Cold War, anticommunism is no longer much of an animating force for Americans to get behind. Do you think there are any overriding issues that everyone can stand up for today? Or do you think society is doomed to be divided in opinion and sympathy?

Nelson Mandela

Manuel Noriega

Operation Desert Storm

Map 951: Note the following places using the map:

Location of Allied central command:

Bodies of water with Allied naval forces:

Countries targeted by Iraqi Scud missiles:

ADA

Clarence Thomas

Sexual harassment

Newt Gingrich

Pic 952: The U.S. lost 148 soldiers in the Gulf War (1990-1991), and 4,425 in the Iraq War (2003-2012). Dividing, what percentage of the deaths in the Iraq War died in the Gulf War?

| Pic 953: Why did the scene in this picture not comport with Bush's promise of "Read my lips, no new taxes?"

Varying Viewpoints 954: How did the following argue regarding the origins of modern conservatism?

Daniel Bell   *Alan Brinkley*

The Edsalls   *Ron Formisano*

Kim Phillips-Fein   *Rick Perlstein*

Lisa McGirr   *Lizabeth Cohen*

Shulman & Cowie   *Critchlow & Dochuk*

At the end of history lies the undiscovered country. In this case, the America of the present and the future. Our America.

Quote 957: What do you think Clinton means here by 'global village'?

_____

Bill Clinton _____

Al Gore _____

DLC _____

Map 958: Although he won zero electoral votes, almost 20,000,000 voted for _____

"Don't ask, don't tell" _____

Pic 958: Bill was the only president to have been a Rhodes scholar, and Hillary was the only First Lady to have also been a U.S. senator, when she ran and won in this state:	In the 1990s, the U.S. lowered its overall violent crime rate, primarily by:

Quote 959: Which demographic was the Newt Gingrich-inspired Contract with America targeting?

_____

Contract with America _____

Oklahoma City bombing _____

Pic 960: How did McVeigh cause all this damage?	What was McVeigh's fate?

Graph 961: While historically the primary source for immigrants coming to the U.S. was Europe, these two places have surpassed Europe since 1970:

_____

Welfare Reform Bill _____

Pg. 962: What are some of the things the Latinos have done to become 'Makers of America?'

_____

_____

Contending Voices 964 - Summarize the views of the following:

Joe Lieberman	Marian Edelman

With whom do you agree more?

Bob Dole

'Soccer moms'

Note how the following affected the affirmative action debate:

Prop. 209	Hopwood v. Texas

Graph 965: The overall pattern reflects increasing	Quote 965: Was Steele for or against affirmative action in principle?
a. urbanization *b. suburbanization*	

Explain why the following deaths agitated race relations so much in the U.S. during the 1990s?

Rodney King death	*Nicole Brown Simpson death*

Pic 966: Clinton gave tax breaks to African American communities in the hope the money would be:	Pic 967: These people fear NAFTA will take away:

NAFTA

WTO

This was not something that helped spur the 1990s boom-time economy for better or worse:

a. Federal Reserve rates   b. Rise of the Internet   c. Deregulation   d. Glass-Steagall Act

Outsourcing

Pic 968: Do you think high levels of immigration to the U.S. while simultaneously outsourcing jobs away from the U.S. is sustainable economically? Why or why not?

Graph 968: Which country had the same percentage of women in the workforce in 2011?	Pics 969: Note some of the new 'firsts' for women in the 1990s:

'Pink-collar ghetto'

How did the increasing participation of women in the U.S. workforce economy affect families?

Summarize the Clinton Administration's response to the following foreign crises during the 1990s:

Somalian warlords   *Rwandan genocide*

Bosnian conflict   *Serb-Albanian conflict*

Rabin-Arafat talks   *Rise of Osama bin Laden and Al Qaeda*

Pic 971: What is the PLO and what were its objectives in the 1990s?

Whitewater

Lewinsky affair

Pic 972: Read and rate this one, which could be about your grandchildren. Why do you like it?

| Pic 973: What was the "Dot-com bubble?"

Map 974: During the 2000 presidential campaign, Al Gore phoned the "most awkward" call in modern history. What was it and why did he make the call?

| Who won the popular vote in 2000?

E Pluribus Unum, a traditional American motto, means *Of Many, One.* Do you think there is a "real American" out there, a way of life, a people, an ideal? Or is the book right to use the term *E Pluribus Plures,* meaning *Of Many, Many* to describe us? In your opinion, can we be "united in diversity?" or are we forever to be divided by it?

How were school curriculums changed at the turn of the century to reflect America's growing multiculturalism?

| Pic 975: How does this building reflect the postmodernist concept?

Postmodernism

Do you agree with the modernists or postmodernists on "less is more" or "less is a bore"?

Pic 976: In *Gone with the Wind,* the slave system was depicted humanely, with good feelings shown between the plantation owning family and the slaves who worked it. What is Kara Walker's message in this artwork on the same topic?

Pic 976 (bot.): Aside from break dancing, think of other aspects of hip-hop culture familiar to you:

Note the themes taken on by the following postmodern writers and rate it 1-3 as in, 1 = Not interesting, will not read, 2 = maybe, need more information and 3 = I might actually read this:

David Foster Wallace　　　　*Colson Whitehead*　　　　*Toni Morrison*

E. Annie Proulx　　　　*Welch/Silko/Harjo/Alexie*　　　　*Amy Tan (Quote 977)*

Ha Jin　　　　*Jhumpa Lahiri*　　　　*Junot Diaz*

Tony Kushner　　　　*Jonathan Larson*　　　　*Eve Ensler*

(Now circle the one you are most likely to seek out in the future)

'Sampling' _____

'Mashup' _____

'Niche logic' _____

In the past there was an American national experience which most people were a part of and which drove and solidified national life. People watched the Thanksgiving Day Parade on TV or went to watch it live. What effect do you think things like the postmodernist attitude to life, audience fragmentation, multiculturalism and a popular culture that often directed at making fun of traditional "America" have on that old national feeling? Do you think it is gone? If it can come back, how? Is it worth bringing back or even remembering?

Quote 979: If Obama is telling Americans to 'grow up' in this statement, what do you think he means?

___

WMDs

George W. Bush (43)

Do you agree or disagree with Bush on the following:

That public money should not be used for stem-cell research: _____

That human cloning should be carefully regulated if not banned: _____

That signing the Kyoto Treaty would have been bad for business: _____

That drilling oil in Alaska is better than in the Middle East: _____

That these things should be done regardless of environment: _____

Dick Cheney

Chart 980: Add the combined U.S. budget deficit for each presidential term in the new millennium:

Bush Term 1: 2001 + 2002 + 2003 + 2004: _____

Bush Term 2: 2005 + 2006 + 2007 + 2008: _____

Obama Term 1: 2009 + 2010 + 2011 + 2012: _____

9/11

Pic 981: Note what happened with each of the three hijacked planes:

Plane 1:   *Plane 2:*   *Plane 3:*

___

Al Qaeda

Taliban

How was 'asymmetrical warfare' different than conventional warfare?

Patriot Act

Dept. of Homeland Security

Guantanamo

Pg. 983: Examining the Evidence. What about U.S. foreign policy does the National Security Strategy illuminate?

'Axis of Evil'

Neoconservatives

Quote 984: Speaking as a prosecutor, what specific charges is Bush laying on Iraq here?	Did Bush listen to the advice of 'old school' conservatives like Colin Powell and Pat Buchanan, or to neoconservative advisors on the Iraq issue?

Bush went to war without the approval of a majority of Democrats and Republicans in Congress:
 	
    a. True   *b. False*
	It was easier to defeat Iraq militarily and depose Saddam Hussein than to remake Iraq into a modern, democratic nation
	
	    a. True *b. False*

Abu Gharib

Map 985: Iraq, the scene of the oldest settled civilizations in the world, has been inhabited for over 5,000 years. Known as Mesopotamia to historians, most of its major cities lie along its two great rivers. Note the battles fought along both rivers:

    Tigris River: *Euphrates River:*

Chart 985: Iran is a Shi'a-majority country. Why might someone looking at this chart not be surprised that after the U.S. withdrawal, Iran's influence in Iraq increased dramatically despite the two countries fighting a war in the 1980s?	Quote 985: Do you agree more with the perspective of Bush the elder or Bush the younger on Iraq? Why?
Pic 986: Do you agree or disagree with these German protesters that oil was a major factor in the Bush administration's decision-making?	Pg. 987: How did British voters reward their pro-American Prime Minister Tony Blair?

No Child Left Behind

In recent elections, a few key 'swing states' have decided the presidency. In 2000 it was Florida. Which state was it in 2004?	Note the social issues Bush took on during his second term:

Hurricane Katrina

FEMA

Nancy Pelosi

Pic 988: Many candidates in the 2016 election season brought up the issue of America's aging infrastructure and its lack of maintenance due to spending in other areas. How might they use this picture to bolster their claim that focus should be placed more on rebuilding the country?	Pic 989: Describe Barack Obama's unique background and state whether you think it helped or hurt his chances in 2008:

Thinking Globally 990 – Note ways the U.S. has been:

Seen as a hyperpower

Seen as a hapless power

Graph 992: How many months did the Dow take to reach 11,500, the point where it was before the real estate bubble burst and the recession struck?

| Note the social consequences of the subprime mortgage bubble bursting:

Deleveraging

TARP

'Toxic' asset

Map 993: How many 'major' states with 15 electoral votes or over went to the following:

Obama: *McCain:*

| Quote 993: Is Obama optimistic or pessimistic about the times here?

'Great Recession'

'Obamacare'

Wall Street Reform and Consumer Protection Act

'Tea Party'

Sonia Sotomayor

Elena Kagan

'Fiscal chicken'

Map 995: What does 'demography is destiny' mean in the context of this electoral map?

Jihadi

Pic 996: Describe the atmosphere in the room where, in this historic photograph, the 'top brass' are watching as U.S. Navy Seal Team Six storms the Bin Laden compound in Pakistan:

'Drones'

Contending Voices 997 - Summarize the views of the following:

Nancy Ripley | *Bennett Weiss*

With whom do you agree more?

'Occupy Wall Street'

| Pic 998: Obama's campaign slogans were, "Change we can believe in" and "Yes we can." Which amendments does the protester on the left *not* want changed? | Who do the "99%" in the other photo want indicted? | If you had to be in either of these pics, which would it be? |

Income gap

Pic 999: Whose fault is it that this lady is being evicted from the home she mortgaged?

a. her fault because she didn't pay her mortgage   *b. the bankers for their predatory lending*

c. the government's fault for not regulating it   *d. maybe a little of all of these*

How many Americans did the iconic company of the mid-20th century, General Motors, employ?

How many does the iconic company of the early-21st century, Apple, employ?

Chart 1000 (top): Which single stat on this chart most surprises you and why?

Chart 1000 (bot.): People who make over 34,823 dollars per year pay this %:

Mitt Romney

Paul Ryan

What was decided in the *Citizens United v. Federal Election Commission* case? | Do you agree with
| the verdict?
|
|

Map 1001: Most counties in the U.S. were   *a. Republican red*   *b. Democrat blue*   in 2012.

The blue voting counties must have   *a. more*   *b. fewer*   *c. the same*   population as the red.

Pic 1002: Do you predict retirees over 65 will have more or | Graph 1003: When pundits say
less political power in the coming decades? Why? | "we are in uncharted territory"
| regarding government spending,
| what do you think they mean?
|
What is an 'unfunded liability?' |
|
|

DREAM Act

In *Arizona v. United States* (2012), the Obama Justice Department under Eric Holder sued the State of Arizona over a law passed which allowed police to question the legal status of someone they were searching, and detain them if they were illegal. The Supreme Court took on the case and ruled in favor of Obama and against Arizona, with the lawyers using the argument that Arizona was encouraging its officers to use racial profiling. What do you think about this ruling?

| What was decided in | Why did same-sex marriage | Why was Obama's NSA
| Shelby County v. Holder? | advocates celebrate in 2012? | criticized?
| |
| |
| |
| |
| |

Pic 1004: Do you agree more with the comic on the left or the right? _____

Pic 1004 (bot.) Do you agree people should show ID when voting? _____

The End! Almost. Carefully read the final page, 1006, *The American Prospect.* Summarize it on the left and state your own opinion on the right. Thanks for doing all this work, to learn about the history of our country. Best wishes in the future, and never give up!
|
|
|
|

Focus on Success Chapter _____   Name _____

Part I: Turn back to the page before the first page of this chapter.
Count the bullet points in the 'Must Understand' section and number that many on this paper; summarize.

Part II: Locate the three prompts in the 'Historical Thinking Skills' section (green box). Write the skill types for this chapter on the lines below, then answer the prompt.

1. _____:

2. _____:

3. _____:

Unit Review Questions for Unit _____   **Name** _____

1.   2.   3.   4.

5.   6.   7.   8.

9.   10.   11.   12.

13.   14.   15.   16.

17.   18.   19.   20.

Short Answers

1a. _____

_____

_____

1b. _____

_____

_____

1c. _____

_____

_____

2a. _____

_____

_____

2b. _____

_____

_____

2c. _____

_____

_____

Addenda:

Other Materials and

About this Series

Crash Course* U.S. History Guide

\# _____   *It's Review Time!*   Name _____

Topic of today's episode _____

As the video goes on, summarize a few of the rapid fire points that were *not* covered in the book that seem important:

What topic or theme did "Thought Bubble" portray in this episode?

Why did Mr. Green get shocked (or not) when he read the mystery document?

What was the correct answer?

How did that item tie in to the material in the chapter?

Was there a 'deep' lesson at the very end? What was it?

Test Correction Guide

Corrector_____

Time to get it right!

Test Name_____

Directions: Identify the numbers of the answers you got wrong on the test and write them:

Number　　**Page in Book**　　**Correct answer (written in the form of a statement using stem of question)**

_____

_____

_____

_____

_____

_____

_____

_____

_____

_____

_____

_____

_____

_____

_____

_____

I got most of these wrong because…

History Movie Review

Reviewer _____

What chapter in the book is this movie most appropriate for? _____

The topic(s) it cover(s): _____

Identify some of the key characters in the movie / documentary that embody concepts in the chapter. Describe how the historical issue(s) affect the storyline in the early part of the film.

_____

_____

_____

_____

What was the "low point" or crisis for the main character(s) in the movie? How did the historical issue cause or influence that low point / crisis to occur?

_____

_____

By the end of the movie, it is probable that whatever crises or effects the historical issue was causing was resolved in some way. Explain how this turn of events came about:

_____

_____

_____

Rate this movie from 0-3: _____
3: it was intellectually stimulating and entertaining
2: it had good points but was rather dull
1: it seemed misleading or irrelevant
0: it was not worth seeing- waste of time

One image or scene that stuck out was:

_____

_____

Why did you rate it the way you did?

_____

_____

Would you recommend this movie to friends or relatives outside of history class?

_____

_____

Weekly Planner

Name _____

This week is number: _____

The Main Objective is: _____

Notes and highlights to keep in mind for the test:

_____

_____

_____

_____

_____

_____

_____

_____

_____

_____

_____

_____

_____

_____

_____

_____

Favorite U.S. History Textbooks

In the 19th century when U.S. history began to be taught in schools in a systematic way, George Bancroft had written the standard work, *History of the United States,* on the Colonial Era and the Revolution up to that time. Edward Channing later wrote a standard work, also called *History of the United States,* going through the Civil War. What follows is a list of the top 10 textbooks since, aside from the Bailey/Kennedy/Cohen text we are familiar with.

1. Boyer, Paul et al. *The Enduring Vision.* 1990 and subsequent editions.
    Another very good U.S. history textbook, also still used

2. Brinkley, Alan, *American History.* 1961 and subsequent editions.
    Key text used as a standard work in colleges for many years

3. Boorstin, Daniel. *The Americans (3 vol.).* 1958.
    A Pulitzer-prize winning history of the country

4. Maurois, Andre. *The Miracle of America.* 1944.
    First came Lafayette, then Tocqueville, and then Maurois

5. Muzzey, David Seville. *A History of Our Country.* 1936.
    Taught more students American history than perhaps any other book

6. Van Loon, Hendrik. *America.* 1927.
    Van Loon won the very first Newbery medal, and does all his own art

7. Beard, Charles A. *The Rise of American Civilization (2 vol.).* 1927.
    Bailey called this book "challenging" and it is, classic college text

8. Markham, Edwin. *The Real America in Romance (9 vol.).* 1909.
    Storybook history. Worth it.

9. Fiske, John. *The New World (3 vol.).* 1902.
    One of the big historians, published after his death in History of All Nations by Lea Brothers. Problem with this it is very hard to find. Good luck.

10. Lossing, Benson, *Lossing's New History of the United States (2 vol.).* 1889.
    Classic 19th century American history read in schools and out.

Also, as an addendum to an addendum, we'll add a 'left' and 'right' history.

Left	Right
Zinn, Howard	Paul Johnson
A People's History of the United States	*A History of the American People*
1980	1999

Thank You!

If this resource book has no use for you, it has no value. We strive to make materials you can actually *use*. No waste, no filler, only usable resources with minimal marginalia aligned with the course for convenience. This is how *Tamm's Textbook Tools* works:

Coursepak A, the *Assignments* series, one you already have, has daily assignments for Monday and Tuesday (or two other days of the week, however you work it). It has the vocab, people and chapter work covered.

Coursepak B, The *Bundle* series, soon available on *Amazon* and elsewhere, has material that can be used other days during the week. This time the focus is reading comp., online activities, multimedia, video clip response forms, short answers, primary sources and free response questions (FRQs).

Coursepak C, The *Crossover* series, is the part of the *Tamm's Textbook Tools* line that stretches across the disciplines. If you teach Social Studies and want to get an integrated curriculum crossover going with the English department, or Math, Science, Liberal Arts, or other area of the school, you would look for the particular *Crossover* workbooks that fit best. All *Crossovers* weave in material from a variety of subjects in the way your subject relates to them.

Look for these and more in the *Tamm's Textbook Tools* series, a low-cost, timesaving way to find high quality, custom materials tailor made to textbooks in many different subjects. Contact the marketing department anytime with suggestions, corrections and any other correspondence at hudsonfla@gmail.com. Find *TTT* on Facebook as well. Spread the word.

Made in the USA
Las Vegas, NV
03 October 2023

78518795R00125